Social Death

Social death occurs when the social existence of a person or group ceases. With an individual, it can occur before or after physical death. Scholars in a wide range of disciplines have applied the concept to very diverse issues – including genocide, slavery, dementia, hospitalisation, and bereavement. Social death relates to social exclusion, social capital, social networks, social roles and social identity, but its theorising is not united – scholars in one field are often unaware of its use in other fields.

This is the first book to bring a range of perspectives together in a pioneering effort to bring to the field conceptual clarity rooted in empirical data. Preceded by an original theoretical discussion of the concept of social death, contributions from the UK, Romania, Sweden and Israel analyse the fourth age, end of life policies, dying alone at home, suicide, photographs on gravestones, bereavement and the agency of dead musicians. This book was originally published as a special issue of *Contemporary Social Science*.

Jana Králová trained in social work in the Czech Republic and is currently completing a sociology Ph.D. on social death at the Centre for Death and Society, Department of Social and Policy Sciences, University of Bath, UK.

Tony Walter is Honorary Professor of Death Studies at the University of Bath, UK. A sociologist, he has written widely on death in society.

Contemporary Issues in Social Science

Series editor: David Canter, University of Huddersfield, UK

Contemporary Social Science, the journal of the **Academy of Social Sciences**, is an interdisciplinary, cross-national journal which provides a forum for disseminating and enhancing theoretical, empirical and/or pragmatic research across the social sciences and related disciplines. Reflecting the objectives of the Academy of Social Sciences, it emphasises the publication of work that engages with issues of major public interest and concern across the world, and highlights the implications of that work for policy and professional practice.

The *Contemporary Issues in Social Science* book series contains the journal's most cutting-edge special issues. Leading scholars compile thematic collections of articles that are linked to the broad intellectual concerns of *Contemporary Social Science*, and as such these special issues are an important contribution to the work of the journal. The series editor works closely with the guest editor(s) of each special issue to ensure they meet the journal's high standards. The main aim of publishing these special issues as a series of books is to allow a wider audience of both scholars and students from across multiple disciplines to engage with the work of *Contemporary Social Science* and the Academy of Social Sciences.

Most recent titles in the series:

Alcohol and Public Policy
Edited by Thom Brooks

Knowledge Mobilisation and Social Sciences
Research Impact and Engagement
Edited by Jon Bannister and Irene Hardill

Protest, Movements, and Dissent in the Social Sciences
A Multidisciplinary Perspective
Edited by Giovanni Travaglino

Social Science Perspectives on Climate Change
Edited by David Canter

Revisiting the Self
Social Science Perspectives
Edited by Charalambos Tsekeris

The Olympic Legacy
Social Scientific Explorations
Edited by Alan Tomlinson

International and Interdisciplinary Insights into Evidence and Policy
Edited by Linda Hantrais, Ashley Thomas Lenihan and Susanne MacGregor

Social Death
Questioning the life-death boundary
Edited by Jana Králová and Tony Walter

Social Death
Questioning the life-death boundary

Edited by
Jana Králová and Tony Walter

LONDON AND NEW YORK

First published 2017
by Routledge
2 Park Square, Milton Park, Abingdon, Oxon, OX14 4RN, UK

and by Routledge
711 Third Avenue, New York, NY 10017, USA

Routledge is an imprint of the Taylor & Francis Group, an informa business

© 2017 Academy of Social Sciences

All rights reserved. No part of this book may be reprinted or reproduced or utilised in any form or by any electronic, mechanical, or other means, now known or hereafter invented, including photocopying and recording, or in any information storage or retrieval system, without permission in writing from the publishers.

Trademark notice: Product or corporate names may be trademarks or registered trademarks, and are used only for identification and explanation without intent to infringe.

British Library Cataloguing in Publication Data
A catalogue record for this book is available from the British Library

ISBN 13: 978-1-138-20530-7

Typeset in Times New Roman
by RefineCatch Limited, Bungay, Suffolk

Publisher's Note
The publisher accepts responsibility for any inconsistencies that may have arisen during the conversion of this book from journal articles to book chapters, namely the possible inclusion of journal terminology.

Disclaimer
Every effort has been made to contact copyright holders for their permission to reprint material in this book. The publishers would be grateful to hear from any copyright holder who is not here acknowledged and will undertake to rectify any errors or omissions in future editions of this book.

Contents

Citation Information	vii
Notes on Contributors	ix
Foreword *David Canter*	xi
1. What is social death? *Jana Králová*	1
2. Agency in the context of social death: dying alone at home *Glenys Caswell and Mórna O'Connor*	15
3. Social death and the moral identity of the fourth age *Chris Gilleard and Paul Higgs*	28
4. Social death in end-of-life care policy *Erica Borgstrom*	38
5. Post-mortem social death – exploring the absence of the deceased *Annika Jonsson*	50
6. To resist or to embrace social death? Photographs of couples on Romanian gravestones *Adela Toplean*	62
7. (Social) Death is not the end: resisting social exclusion due to suicide *Zohar Gazit*	76
8. The agency of dead musicians *Lisa McCormick*	89
Index	103

Citation Information

The chapters in this book were originally published in *Contemporary Social Science*, volume 10, issue 3 (September 2015). When citing this material, please use the original page numbering for each article, as follows:

Chapter 1
What is social death?
Jana Králová
Contemporary Social Science, volume 10, issue 3 (September 2015) pp. 235–248

Chapter 2
Agency in the context of social death: dying alone at home
Glenys Caswell and Mórna O'Connor
Contemporary Social Science, volume 10, issue 3 (September 2015) pp. 249–261

Chapter 3
Social death and the moral identity of the fourth age
Chris Gilleard and Paul Higgs
Contemporary Social Science, volume 10, issue 3 (September 2015) pp. 262–271

Chapter 4
Social death in end-of-life care policy
Erica Borgstrom
Contemporary Social Science, volume 10, issue 3 (September 2015) pp. 272–283

Chapter 5
Post-mortem social death – exploring the absence of the deceased
Annika Jonsson
Contemporary Social Science, volume 10, issue 3 (September 2015) pp. 284–295

Chapter 6
To resist or to embrace social death? Photographs of couples on Romanian gravestones
Adela Toplean
Contemporary Social Science, volume 10, issue 3 (September 2015) pp. 296–309

CITATION INFORMATION

Chapter 7

(Social) Death is not the end: resisting social exclusion due to suicide
Zohar Gazit
Contemporary Social Science, volume 10, issue 3 (September 2015) pp. 310–322

Chapter 8

The agency of dead musicians
Lisa McCormick
Contemporary Social Science, volume 10, issue 3 (September 2015) pp. 323–335

For any permission-related enquiries please visit:
http://www.tandfonline.com/page/help/permissions

Notes on Contributors

Erica Borgstrom is a lecturer at the Open University, UK. She is an anthropologist with an interest in medical issues and dying studies. Her work explores end-of-life care policy and the experiences of those living with chronic and/ or terminal illness.

Glenys Caswell is a research fellow at the University of Nottingham, UK. Her research interests centre on the social context of death and dying, with a particular focus on exploring what constitutes a good death and examining the perceived need for dying people to be accompanied.

Zohar Gazit recently completed his PhD in the Department of Sociology and Anthropology at the Hebrew University of Jerusalem, Israel. His doctoral dissertation examined social organisations promoting alternative perceptions and practices concerning death in Israeli society.

Chris Gilleard is visiting research fellow in the Division of Psychiatry at University College London, UK, and a Fellow of the Academy of Social Sciences. His interests are in the history, psychology and sociology of ageing and old age. He is the co-author of *Ageing, Corporeality and Embodiment* (2013).

Paul Higgs is Professor of the Sociology of Ageing at University College London, UK, and the editor of the journal *Social Theory and Health*. He is the co-author of *Rethinking Old Age: Theorising the Fourth Age* (2015) and co-editor of *Ageing and Social Class* (2013).

Annika Jonsson is a lecturer in sociology at Karlstad University, Sweden. Her research interests include the social psychology of continuing bonds, the role of continuing bonds in post-secular cultures, and death as a practical accomplishment in late modern society.

Jana Králová trained in social work in the Czech Republic and is currently completing a sociology Ph.D. on social death at the Centre for Death and Society, Department of Social and Policy Sciences, University of Bath, UK.

Lisa McCormick is Lecturer in Sociology at the University of Edinburgh, UK. She is the author of *Performing Civility: International Competitions in Classical Music* (2015), and co-editor of *Myth, Meaning and Performance: Toward a New Cultural Sociology of the Arts* (with Ron Eyerman, 2006).

Mórna O'Connor has a background in psychology and is currently undertaking a PhD at the University of Nottingham, UK, exploring the experiences of bereaved people in Internet-era mourning.

Adela Toplean is New Europe College Research Fellow and Assistant Professor in the Faculty of Letters at the University of Bucharest, Romania. Her research interests range from the

NOTES ON CONTRIBUTORS

sociology of religion and of the sacred, to the sociology of death and epistemological grounds of thanatology.

Tony Walter is a sociologist and Honorary Professor of Death Studies at the University of Bath, UK. He is currently writing three new books: *Death: Contemporary Challenges* (Policy Press), *Death in the Modern World* (Sage), and *Living with the Dead in the 21st Century* (Routledge).

Foreword

Is it possible to be dead whilst still alive? By contrast is it possible to be alive while being dead? Social scientists are exploring these apparent oxymorons by invoking the notion of *social death*. As Jana Kralova, from the University of Bath, argues in the present volume devoted to the topic, the study of social death is now exploring many different forms of existence.

Perhaps the clearest example of a person being socially dead is given by Glenys Caswell and Morna O'Connor at the University of Nottingham. They describe the rare, but not unknown, example of a man they call Adam Jackson whose skeletal remains were found in his house at least four years after his death. This man had apparently been living so isolated an existence that his absence from any social contact was only noticed when a bailiff broke into Mr Jackson's house because of unpaid bills. I suppose it could be argued that he had a social existence long after death because of the bills he was amassing, but social death had occurred much earlier during his life when he disappeared from interaction with anyone else.

Caswell and O'Connor propose that Mr Jackson may have chosen a degree of isolation equivalent to social death for his own, possibly rational, reasons. They argue that although this was his right it is frowned on by society at large. This leads to the irony that the public concern with his lonely death gave him a social existence after his body was found. An existence promoted further by Caswell and O'Connor's own researches.

Although Adam Jackson may have had an acceptable rationale for his isolation, for many others social death may be wished on them unwillingly. This is illustrated by Chris Gilleard and Paul Higgs of University College London when they discuss the ways that conceptualisations of dementia may inadvertently treat people as if they are socially dead. They consider this in the context of notions of a fear of a fourth age in which the loss of agency associated with frailty, especially mental frailty, can set a person, as Gilleard and Higgs put it, 'on an undignified journey towards non-existence'. By recognising the risk of this pathway to social death they point to the significance for carers in maintaining their relationship with the person cared for so that those carers themselves are protected from the depersonalising aspects of the fourth age.

Where a person is known to be terminally ill there is also a risk of social death before physical death. This is examined by Erica Borgstrom from the London school of Hygiene and Tropical Medicine. She focuses on end-of-life care policies in England. These emphasise the importance of actively involving the dying person in planning for their death in order to reduce the risk of them becoming non-persons. Such an approach challenges the medicalisation of death, with its focus on the body. As in so many other areas of medicine, the person is put in the background. Their agency is subordinate to their body as a case to be managed.

A particularly powerful challenge to social death comes from a context in which dominant public attitudes, encouraged by religious belief systems, commit a dead person to being non-existent in social discourse because the person committed suicide. This, perhaps unexpectedly in a modern, essentially liberal democracy is the case in Israel. As discussed by Zohar Gazit of the

FOREWORD

Hebrew University of Jerusalem, orthodox Judaism considers suicide taboo and this is reflected in general attitudes and behaviours. As a consequence a movement is growing in Israel seeking to have suicide recognised as a social problem. In particular the social death that typically accompanies suicide is highlighted with the aim of drawing attention to survivors' entitlement to consideration and support. An important aspect of this is the way the social death of a person who commits suicide hides the issues that gave rise to suicide and therefore reduces the possibility of dealing with those issues in order to prevent further suicides.

The post-mortem social death associated with suicide also opens up the possibility of post-mortem life. As Annika Jonsson from Karlstad University illustrates in the present volume, there are many ways in which the dead are kept alive, at least in the minds and social processes of the living. She shows how this operates in Sweden, where one in five claim to have been in contact with or sensed the presence of a deceased. This contact also often takes the form of storytelling about the deceased. This allows continuing bonds to exist that keeps the dead person within the community. These can be strong bonds, in which the deceased is still considered to have an important significance in the lives of survivors. Or the bonds can be non-existent, due for example, to a lack of knowledge about earlier generations, perhaps made worse by a move from a long-established family home. In this case there is post-mortem social death.

Adela Toplean from the University of Bucharest explores a particularly intriguing way in which couples in Romania ward of post-mortem social death. Photographs of the couple are put on the gravestones of the first to die. Toplean argues that this has roots in Romanian Orthodox Christianity's acceptance of material aspects of belief through Icons, veneration of relics and a widespread view that photographs contain an aspect of the person. The photographs of couples therefore continue the bonds between the living and the dead. The public nature of these photographs allows an intimacy with the dead outside the home. As Toplean says, within the religious and cultural context of Romania, these photographs are an active shield against the process of social dying.

Perhaps the clearest example of post-mortem life is the way famous composers live on in many different ways. Lisa McCormick from the University of Edinburgh reveals this in the power of what she calls 'the agency of dead musicians'. McCormick discusses how composers are venerated through commemorative rites, notably anniversary programming. But it is the tangible object of the musical score that gives famous composers the edge on post-mortem longevity. The inevitable ambiguity of music notation provides a spur to search for what composers 'really want'. This quest limits the impact of social death.

Just as Adam Jackson comes alive again in the present volume, and the surviving members of married couples in Romania relive their marriage through a photograph with their partner on a gravestone, so the Path to Life in Israel fights the social death that blights suicide there. These all illustrate the importance of recognising the possibility of social death and its consequences, so effectively encapsulated by Jana Kralova and Tony Walter in editing this volume.

Professor David Canter
Series Editor

What is social death?

Jana Králová

Department of Social and Policy Sciences, Centre for Death and Society, University of Bath, Bath, UK

Social death is on many occasions used too broadly by academics in several different disciplines, creating ambiguity around its application. Conceptual clarification is needed, not least because of the importance of the empirical topics to which the concept has been applied, such as genocide, slavery and dementia. Analysis of repeatedly occurring structural similarities in diverse studies of social death reveals three underlying notions: a loss of social identity, a loss of social connectedness and losses associated with disintegration of the body. The article concludes firstly, that social death is a multifaceted phenomenon with a single conceptual framework; secondly, that in order to preserve the concept's theoretical potential it should only be used for the most extreme circumstances whereby most or all of the key facets are severely compromised and/or lost; thirdly, that social death might be usefully seen as the opposite of well-being, so that well-being and social death each clarify the meaning of the other.

Introduction

What is social death? The term has been used by a wide range of scholars from different disciplines, working in different substantive fields, and – this article argues – not entirely consistently. The need for conceptual clarity is highlighted by the increasing, but often varied, use of the term. In the past six years, three substantial academic books (Cacho, 2012; Guenther, 2013; Norwood, 2009) have been published with social death in their title or subtitle. After briefly sketching the history of social science's use of 'social death', the article analyses some key studies using the concept in order to identify its central components.

The term 'social death' first entered social science vocabulary with Sudnow's (1967) study of social processes surrounding death. It was based on observations from two hospitals, where he described how the presumed social value of patients near death determines how they are treated by medical personnel and how much effort is invested into reviving them. He spelled out the differences between clinical, biological and social death. This is conducted through the actions of others whereby they treat the person as already deceased, although still clinically and biologically alive. However, a more commonly cited study that implies a distinction between physical and social death is Glaser and Strauss (1966). They describe how awareness of a person's dying determines social interaction. They build their understanding of social death on Goffman's (1961) concept of mortification of self – the series of humiliations undermining a person's social identity as observed in a mental hospital. Kalish (1968) reconceptualised death as physical, psychological, sociological and social, and distinguished self-perceived social death, where a person believes that they are as good as dead, from other-perceived social death where it is others who think this.

Sweeting and Gilhooly (1991) comprehensively review social death literature in sociology and nursing. Later, they (1997) interviewed caregiving relatives of dementia sufferers, finding discrepancies between the carer's belief and their behaviour concerning their relative's social death. Of 95 caregivers, over a third believed and behaved as if their relative were socially dead, while more than another third neither believed nor behaved as if their relative were socially dead. Interestingly, one-fifth believed that their relative was socially dead while themselves behaving otherwise, and only four carers treated their relative as socially dead while believing in their social existence.

In histories of slavery the concept of social death is commonly attributed to Patterson (1982) who does not, however, cite any of the above-mentioned previous studies. Within a context of authority and alienation, he proposes two conceptions of social death – *intrusive* and *extrusive* – depending on how the slaves were initially recruited. In the intrusive mode, 'the slave was ritually incorporated as the permanent enemy on the inside – the "domestic enemy" […]' (Patterson, 1982, p. 39). In the extrusive mode:

> the dominant image of the slave was that of an insider who had fallen, one who ceased to belong and had been expelled from normal participation in the community because of a failure to meet certain minimal legal or socioeconomic norms of behaviour. (Patterson, 1982, p. 41)

His concept of *liminal incorporation*, derived from Van Gennep (1960) and Turner (1967), suggests that slaves were still part of society although socially dead. He then discusses the slaves' *natal alienation*, loss of connection not only with past but also with possible future generations. It is this loss of cross-generational links, of cultural heritage as well as a sense of belonging to a place that became key for later studies of genocide. Hence Claudia Card argues for adding the social death concept to the UN definition of genocide (2010). She quotes Patterson's (1982) definition of social death that captures the non-existence of a slave outside of their master, their dislocation from community and their natal alienation from the family/tribe they were born to. Additionally, she recognises other forms of social death such as 'slavery, banishment, disfigurement, illness, even self-chosen isolation' (2010, p. 237).

Thus the general trend among scholars using the social death concept is to use it when a person/group has experienced extreme and profound loss. Death studies and gerontology concentrate on loss of role, of social identity, of social capital and of social networks; refugee studies examine displacement, social exclusion, loss of citizenship, of economic capital and of access to resources; slavery studies look at interplay of power dynamics and examine the loss of cultural capital and of links across the generations, on which genocide studies also draw. Scholars also consider the withdrawal of legal protection, as with prisoners, and the severe impact of this on their health. The focus of each interdisciplinary substantive field differs depending on its subject matter. This results in social death meaning the loss of one or more of the above named facets. However, people can suffer most of these losses simultaneously, though the extent of their losses differs according to individual circumstances.

For example, consider war refugees. In order to save their lives they are forced to leave their country of origin, losing access to their cultural heritage, cross-generational links, social networks, social as well as economic capital and roles associated with family and employment. Their human rights are endangered, while their stigmatised status entails social exclusion, all of which severely impacts on their mental and physical health. This, however, may be mitigated if at least some of these facets remain, despite the circumstances. Those Jews fleeing to the USA in the 1930s were often integrated into existing Jewish communities and also gained citizenship, depending on their social, economic and cultural capital. This leads us to consider what are the key facets of social death and at what point social death occurs.

In order to clarify the conceptual boundaries of social death, scholars need to agree on a unified conceptual framework and establish the point at which persons/groups will be considered socially dead. This article aims to start this process, at the same time showing where the special issue articles lie within the social death scholarship (the earlier articles discuss social death before physical death, the later ones social death after physical death).

Methods

The empirical investigation of social death is problematic for several reasons: the physical and social inaccessibility of the socially dead; concern about the well-being of those deemed socially dead as well as of the researchers; and the risk of losing other theoretical possibilities for the concept should the research be limited to only one substantive academic area in which the socially dead exist. All of these in turn provide a rationale for theoretical inquiry into the concept of social death.

In their extensive review of literature on conceptual frameworks, Leshem and Trafford (2007) concluded that constructing conceptual frameworks helps academics to reveal theories underpinning research and to capture dynamics between them. It also informs what methods are chosen to conduct any inquiry, thus creating transparency of the research process. I would add that it is possible to access an ethically problematic area of inquiry more easily if one explores it theoretically.

In order to identify and unify social death's theoretical boundaries, therefore, something beyond a literature review is needed, namely a systematic comparison across disciplines of the concepts on which social death rests. Varying levels of theoretical development across as well as within the relevant disciplines requires applying both inductive and deductive inquiry. Sometimes concepts need to be compared with one another, at other times primary empirical incidents examined across different studies allowing us to establish their similarities, differences and relationships. Out of this will emerge higher order concepts that allow the development of an overarching conceptual framework. This approach to analysis/synthesis has much in common with meta-ethnography:

> Meta-ethnography seeks to go beyond single accounts to reveal the analogies between the accounts. It reduces the accounts while preserving the sense of the account through the selection of key metaphors and organizers. The 'senses' of different accounts are then translated into one another. The analogies revealed in these translations are the form of the meta-ethnographic synthesis. (Noblit & Hare, 1988, p. 13)

My research has involved a systematic approach: searching for data (Booth, Papaioannou, & Sutton, 2012), analysis (Boeije, 2002), comparison (Fram, 2013) and synthesis (Noblit & Hare, 1988) using recently developed strategies (Atkins et al., 2008). The following databases were searched for the term 'social death' using Boolean operators with the following results: Web of Science 120, Social Policy and Practice 5, SCOPUS 125, PsychNet 65, PubMed 32 and IBSS 56 by June 2015. Due to limited resources only the studies from IBSS were analysed and seminal studies derived from a screening of their reference lists were also read.

This article, however, will present only studies relevant to the three identified facets, and begin to sketch social death's conceptual framework. Its primary features will be a loss of social identity, of social connectedness and those losses associated with the disintegration of the body.

Loss of social identity

For the purposes of the following discussion, I shall take identity to refer to

> the way people understand themselves in relation to other persons, to the world around them and to supernatural realms. Identity is a consequence of self-consciousness with particular social networks embedded within a particular language. Throughout life, the relationships which grow between individual men, women and children, as members of families and society, help foster that sense of who they are and of their purpose in the world. (Davies, 2002, p. 4)

The following section will discuss notions of the 'non-person' (Goffman, 1961), 'homo sacer' (Agamben, 1998) and the 'ex-human' (Biehl, 2004), revealing structural similarities and differences in these concepts and using them as a theoretical springboard to explain the loss of social identity that is embedded in the concept of social death.

Goffman's (1961) essay on the situation of mental hospital patients revealed the processes involved in long-term hospitalisation which result in a person's institutionalisation. This is achieved through the ongoing process of disculturation, where the person is not only removed from their natural social setting, causing them to lose their social roles, but is also placed in the institution's degrading environment which initially removes all significant components of the individuals' identity, forcing them to become a 'non-person'. '[T]he recruit comes into the establishment with a conception of himself made possible by certain stable social arrangements in his home world [...]; upon entrance, he is immediately stripped of the support provided by these arrangements' and then 'begins a series of abasements, degradations, humiliations, and profanations of self' (Goffman, 1961, p. 24). Furthermore, the person placed in such an institution would often also acquire a stigma (Goffman, 1963).

A similar notion of absolute loss of a person's value can be observed in Ancient Roman law, where as a form of punishment the status of 'homo sacer' was inflicted upon those who had committed a crime (Agamben, 1998). This entailed indefinite withdrawal of all legal, social and cultural protection, and meant such individuals could be killed at any time by anyone, without the perpetrator being charged. Furthermore, these individuals could never be sacrificed, their death being excluded from any religious context. Therefore, this status leaves a being with what Agamben (1998) calls a 'bare life': unprotected by law and exposed to death at any given time.

Agamben (1998) explains that the status of homo sacer is based on the notion of *inclusive exclusion*: *inclusive* because it marks the person as an 'easy target'. It *stigmatises* it, as if calling out to others, 'you can hurt me, you can kill me, nobody will care', or alternatively, 'when I die, no one will cry' (Hecht, 1998, p. 145). It marks people out just as yellow stars marked out Jews in the Holocaust, prostitutes are vulnerable to rape, and the enemy's children, women, elderly and disabled are susceptible to extreme cruelty in war (Card, 2010). This inclusion means turning irreversibly into a 'non-person' (Goffman, 1961).

The *exclusive* notion refers to segregation from the community and its resources. In Ancient Rome this implied unavoidable death and in some contemporary circumstances it still does (Dageid & Duckert, 2008). The homo sacer's stigma and total lack of protection inexorably exploited their vulnerability, leading to their total social abandonment. In Noys (2005, p. 19) words, 'the exclusion of the criminal from the community seems to cost them their humanity and leave them as nothing more than bare life, something monstrous that exists between the animal and the human, also referred to as subhuman'. So it is that Agamben's (1998) inclusive exclusion resembles the stigmatisation followed by exclusion suggested by Goffman (1961), and chimes with Kellehear's (2007) idea of fear from association with the stigmatised. Furthermore, Patterson's (1982) *intrusive mode* of social death suggests a similar dynamic, where slaves were removed from their context of origin and introduced to the master's household as a 'non-person'. Even so, there is still a difference between the concepts of 'non-person' and 'homo sacer': the first appears to be punished unintentionally, whereas the second is an intended punishment.

Biehl's (2004, p. 476) rich ethnographic description from southern Brazil of Vita, a 'precarious rehabilitation centre for drug addicts and alcoholics', reveals how social death may look on the community level. In this community of 'ex-humans', those who have fallen through the net of social protection, the very poor, people with disabilities, HIV/AIDS and terminal diseases, have been excluded from the wider community to experience an undignified death. He writes, 'Vita is a place in the world for people who have, de facto, been stripped of their humanity and terminally excluded from reality. Before biological death, they experience social death' (Biehl, 2004, p. 476). Thus, 'Vita is indeed the end situation on the road of poverty, the place where the unwanted become unknowables' (Biehl, 2004, p. 477). Biehl (2004) refers to Mauss (1979, p. 80, emphasis original), who argued that it is possible for literal death of an otherwise healthy person to occur simply '[...] *because they know or believe* (which is the same thing) *that they are going to die*'. Thus Biehl (2004, p. 491) argues that 'in the face of increasing economic and biomedical inequality and the breakdown of family structures human bodies are routinely separated from their normal political status and abandoned to the most extreme misfortunes'. Thus his understanding of social death is multidimensional and includes exclusion from a community of belonging, economic vulnerability, withdrawal/weakening of legal protection, stigma and loss of social identity. All this leads to a person anticipating approaching death. An example in this issue might be Gazit's (2015) analysis of the experience of Israelis bereaved by suicide who have either to suffer ostracism by their community of belonging or to remain silent about their loss – both resulting in shame on the identity of the deceased and the bereaved.

Furthermore, Steele, Kidd, and Castano's (2015) recent psychological study 'On social death: ostracism and the accessibility of death thoughts' confirms that ostracism increases thoughts of death. This links neatly to Durkheim's (1951) classical work on suicide, where he proposed that greater social integration among Catholics results in lower suicide rates, compared to Protestants. Nevertheless, an 'ex-human' has many characteristics of a 'non-person' as well as of 'homo sacer', especially through stripping a person of their social identity, self-worth and belonging to a community. The difference remains in how the person arrived at their social death. In the case of Biehl's (2004) 'ex-human', the main trigger is their economic failure, which recalls Patterson's (1982) *extrusive mode* of social death, where the person became a slave due to their inability to fulfil legal or socio-economic norms.

To conclude, these concepts of the 'non-person' (Goffman, 1961), 'homo-sacer' (Agamben, 1998) and 'ex-human' (Biehl, 2004) suggest a loss of social identity and of social integration, triggered by a person's inadequacy in the eyes of others. Here the person's characteristics go hand in hand with their low socio-economic status, leading to social exclusion. This happens simultaneously on several dimensions and may result in the person's physiological death. However, the reasons for this process vary and may include embodied characteristics, personality traits, belief and value systems and/or low economic, social or cultural capital. Physical death is intentional only in the case of 'homo sacer' where it was a means of punishment, while for the 'non-person' this removal was underpinned by the idea of protecting others from the person themselves. 'Ex-humans' have ceased to fulfil societal expectations with regard to their economic status. For all three concepts the process of social abandonment is reinforced by the fear of stigma by association (Goffman, 1963), so that it can be inferred that social death is a consequence of these externally inflicted abandonments causing harm to the person/s and/or groups.

Yet there are some life situations where severe loss of identity and withdrawal from human interaction is a choice made by the person/group. These, however, must not be mistaken for social death. *Disengagement Theory* (Cumming & Henry, 1961), an original although at the time controversial proposal, may serve as an example, in which it was argued that older people's withdrawal from society towards the end of their lives may not only be voluntary, but also functional and mutual.

Similarly, should the person decide to live/die alone by choice, as robustly argued in this issue by Caswell and O'Connor (2015), this would not amount to social death. This is because the person's action results from their autonomy, agency and choice. Likewise, should a person decide to live the monastic life, with no social contact with the outside world, this does not amount to social death either, assuming that they made an informed and voluntary choice to do so, in which case their inner well-being (White, Gaines, & Jha, 2014) is likely to be high while acquiring a new group to belong to. Thus, using the three concepts 'non-person', 'homo sacer' and 'ex-human', we can say that loss of social identity represents one of the core losses embedded in social death.

Loss of social connectedness

Because human beings are inherently social, losing meaningful social connections and roles are likely to be devastating. The most extreme example of externally imposed social isolation is solitary confinement. In her powerful critique of this inhumane form of punishment, Guenther (2013, p. xi) writes: 'There are many ways to destroy a person, but one of the simplest and most devastating is through prolonged solitary confinement. Deprived of meaningful human interaction, otherwise healthy prisoners become unhinged.' This section will consider the basis of social connectedness, its impact on a person's life and death, how a person can cease to be part of society before as well as after their actual death. The social role and profile of the person as they change throughout the life course will be discussed, as will the effects of their loss.

Although social connectedness does not necessarily have to be tied to formal roles, role loss appears in social science literature in, for example, Chambre's (1984) study of volunteering and Moen, Erickson, and Dempster-McClain's (2000) discussion of continuing care. Although role identities may change over a lifetime, some role losses can be long lasting, such as those associated with long-term unemployment (Jahoda & Zeisel, 1972), parenthood (Mulkay & Ernst, 1991), widowhood (Silverman, 2004) or retirement (Moen et al., 2000). The main role in the person's productive life is associated with employment. Jahoda and Zeisel (1972) describe in great detail the impact of long-term unemployment on private as well as community life in the Austrian village of Marienthal, with its decline of community life evidenced by the lack of libraries, neglect of public spaces, lack of participation in political activities and shutting down of nurseries. This all suggests the breakdown of community life. Similarly, the disintegration of interpersonal relationships and people's social identity is obvious in those Marienthal families described as resigned, unbroken, broken or apathetic.

Likewise, Kalish (1968) captures role loss and the breakdown of people's social connectedness in a description which, although dated, reflects what is still a reality for some:

> Thus father is shipped off to a nursing home, where the only concrete evidence of his existence is monthly bills and Christmas cards; his role as father has ceased and no replacement roles exist. He is socially dead in varying degrees to the members of his family whose rejection of him may induce self-perceived social death; this in turn may precipitate or at least hurry psychological and physical death. (p. 255)

Here we again recall Steele et al. (2015) whose study shows how ostracism increases the occurrence of death thoughts, while Seale (1998, p. 170) points out that the prospect of institutionalisation is seen by some as 'an act of social burial'. However, an interesting counterargument is provided in this issue by Gilliard and Higgs (2015) who suggest that despite widespread equating of frail old age with a 'black hole' and dementia with social death, these groups of people can remain socially alive, not least because of their carers' active involvement (Sweeting & Gilhooly, 1997), partly mitigating the unchosen circumstances in which these people may find themselves.

At this point it is important to recognise that losing just one major role, for example, being a parent, is unlikely to cause social death. While an only child's death is a profound loss and may also mean losing social roles associated with parenthood and socially isolating both parents, it remains a loss of only one of many social roles they are likely to inhabit. Bauby (1998) in his autobiographical account of locked-in syndrome provides an outstanding illustration of remaining connected, carving out new roles and identities even when the options for doing so are severally compromised. The question thus remains: What is left of the person in solitary confinement where they lose most or all social roles, their social identity is severely threatened, their ability to maintain meaningful connections with the outside world is non-existent and where the person's existential core is severally destabilised (Guenther, 2013)?

Just as it is possible to turn the living into the socially dead, could the dead remain socially alive? Unruh (1983) discussed strategies that the bereaved use in order to preserve the deceased's identity. These strategies include: (a) reinterpreting the mundane about the deceased, (b) redefining the negative about them, (c) sanctifying meaningful symbols and (d) continuing bonding activities. All of these could preserve not only cultural heritage and a sense of self and belonging, but also ongoing, meaningful relationships with the dead. This notion was initially proposed by Moss and Moss (1985) in their research with elderly widow(er)s. Its conceptual structure was further elaborated by Mulkay and Ernst (1991), finally to be termed *continuing bonds* by Klass, Silverman, and Nickman (1996). All of this severally blurs the boundaries between life and death while extending social connections 'to both sides of the grave' (Mulkay & Ernst, 1991, p. 178).

In this issue, Toplean's (2015) study of a small-scale Transylvanian community examines the traditional practice of family photographs on gravestones. Here, married couples – one person deceased, the other bereaved – are depicted together. This, she argues, resists the social death of the bereaved party. In the light of the theories presented above, it also maintains the social identity of the deceased. Also in this issue, Jonsson (2015), exploring continuing bonds in Sweden, argues that not all deceased remain connected to the living. The living may not wish to continue the relationship or not be able to, resulting in – for them – the ending of the deceased's social existence. The bereaved may find this painful, liberating or to be disregarded. This inverse function of the continuing bonds, assigning agency to the dead, is suggested in this issue by McCormick (2015). She explores the cult of the dead composer in classical music and the fetishisation of deceased vocalists in opera, concluding that relics such as recordings, death masks and physical remains link past and present, while anniversary programmes serve as commemorative rites reinforcing this link. Similarly, Jamieson (1995) uniquely connected social death with material culture in archaeology. Archaeological evidence of African-American burial practices before 1800 suggests that many slaves practised the burial traditions of their group of origin, thus challenging Patterson's (1982) argument that slaves were totally divorced from their cultural heritage. Regardless of their oppression, American slaves retained sufficient autonomy to maintain 'continuing bonds' (Klass et al., 1996) with their culture of origin. Jamieson's (1995) evidence allows Unruh's (1983) four strategies for preserving the identity of and emotional attachment with the dead *to be extended to those living under severe oppression*. Thus, this empirical evidence suggests complex interactional processes between the living and the dead, significantly blurring the life–death divide.

To conclude, life roles are never static and are crucial to a person's social existence. Their loss can have a profound impact on a person's quality of life and ability to connect with their social universe. Moreover, social connections need not cease to exist with the biological death of the person who may or may not be able to secure their continuous identity post-mortem. Nevertheless, for it to amount to social death, I would argue, most or all of the social roles and connections of the person or group would have to be lost.

Losses associated with the body's disintegration

The powerless body

Our social identity is inevitably connected to, and enacted through, our bodies (Hockey & Draper, 2005). This is most visible when it is disintegrating, whether due to illness, old age, abortion, torture, suicide or genocide. Some additional theoretical concepts are considered in the following section to highlight the role of the body in social death.

Borgstrom's (2015) analysis in this issue of English End of Life care policy revealed that it is underpinned by the discourse of social death as conceptualised by hospital ethnographers (Glaser & Strauss, 1966; Sudnow, 1967), so that social death's occurrence prior to a person's physical death is seen as undesirable. As the policy suggests – rightly or wrongly – this can be mitigated by person's agency. Furthermore, this policy promotes social death's prevention by appropriate social relating by healthcare personal. What is striking about Borgstrom's (2015) analysis is an alternative interpretation of what family members or even policy-makers may see as an inhumane treatment. This, she argues, results from the body's dominance in the biomedical model of care, which is responsible for the medical preoccupation with the body rather than with the dying person's disintegrating social universe. This ironically resonates with, but does not prevent, social death whereby the person is treated as a corpse (Sudnow, 1967), their existence reduced to their body.

Similarly, Seale's (1998) notion of *falling from culture* highlights that we enter the world with a physical body that over time becomes increasingly social; at life's end, social roles may collapse and we become just a body to be fed, watered and toileted, implying that '[…] dying men and women today will "die" not once, but many times' (Kellehear, 2007, p. 219). Social connections and social identities are disrupted, the body disintegrates and the person fails to fulfil their usual social interactions. The privacy, social participation, independence and decision-making through which the person's life was once shaped are now threatened by their body's complex disintegration. Thus in dying the body's profound deterioration undermines its owner's social identity, preventing social interaction and disgusting others – what Kellehear (2007) terms *shameful dying*.

Powerful body

A body deteriorated due to very old age, dementia or cancer, although frail, can still possess a certain amount of autonomy and its owner strive to maintain a meaningful social identity. The deteriorating body's remaining resources can be used to resist in ways that are not only powerful but also intractable. Feigning deafness or defecating in sinks and corridors may serve as examples. Other forms of identity-sustaining agency include caring for those who are worse off in their condition than oneself, while avoiding those who are by comparison doing better. There are also positive examples of embodied skills and practices from earlier life that can be applied in some new way. This might be a resident-led 'choir' of inarticulate and physically disabled residents (Hallam, Hockey, & Howarth 1999). The body, however, also possesses the ability to destroy itself through self-harming (Beauboeuf-Lafontant, 2005) or suicide (Agamben, 1998). The body's deterioration due to oppression by others can be observed in starvation from hunger due to unemployment (Jahoda & Zeisel, 1972), prisoners' hunger strikes (Smith, 2013) and the state's systemic failure to provide social protection (Giroux, 2011).

In conclusion, the body, encouraged by its owner's agency, may become an effective tool for sustaining or ending personal identity. Thus it may be asked at what point do bodies become socially dead. Is it when they lose their social identity? Or is it when they are lost or no longer remembered? Or neither? What was it that happened to Doc Daneeka in Catch 22 (Heller, 1955) when, following a plane crash, he was thought to be dead while remaining alive though feeling as good as dead (Gregory & Lewis, 1975)? What is it that adds additional disgrace to the unmarked grave of a criminal? Is it connected to whatever motivates us to create Unknown Soldiers' graves? And how can excavating mass graves help with societal rebuilding after violent conflict (Juhl & Olsen, 2006)? Is it possible for a physiologically functioning body, perhaps in a long-term coma, with dementia, or indeed the healthy body of a refugee, to be socially less significant than a particular physiologically dead body, like that of Lenin displayed in Moscow (McCormick, 2015)? And if this is so, where does responsibility lie for the harm caused to the living? Conversely, in what sense can harm be done to the dead? This remains to be answered.

Thus far I have presented three kinds of loss that, together, I argue amount to some of social death's conceptual base. However, this does not present a complete conceptual framework of social death, as this may only be achieved through more extensive inquiry across many substantive fields of research.

Furthermore, the presented data cannot tell us at what point individuals or groups become socially dead. In order to sharpen social death's conceptual boundaries the following section will present genocide as a most extreme example of social death (Card, 2010) and then juxtapose emerging conceptual properties of social death with those of well-being. The question then arises as to whether social death (although possibly under a different name) could be understood and used as the opposite of 'well-being'.

Demarcation lines: social death and well-being

How can we establish at what point a person or group is socially dead? How many of all of the possible facets of social death (when fully identified) would have to cease, or nearly cease, to exist to amount to social death? Are some of these facets more important than others? Are they interdependent? Is it possible for some to be only partially socially dead (Jonsson, 2015)? In which case are they dead or not? Is there a total social death (Jonsson, 2015)? And is this a helpful way of describing someone's life/death circumstances? Or are there perhaps some other concepts which could serve or are already serving as a better descriptor of such a complex, multidimensional, relational series of losses? And if so, why does social death remain theoretically and analytically attractive?

To begin drawing the demarcation line of social death I will firstly consider genocide as conceptualised by Card (2010) and use it as the most extreme example of social death. Secondly, I will juxtapose social death with well-being and ask whether social death may be usefully seen as the opposite of well-being so that well-being and social death each clarify the meaning of the other.

'Genocide is social death' asserts Card (2010, p. 237), for whom the antithesis of social death is *social vitality.* This

> exists through relationships, contemporary and intergenerational, that create contexts and identities that give meaning and shape to our lives. Some of those relationships are with kin, friends, and co-workers. Others are less personal and mediated by basic social institutions – economic, political, religious, educational, and so on. Loss of social vitality comes with the loss of such connections. (Card, 2010, p. 237)

Furthermore, '[s]ocial vitality is interpersonal. An individual can experience social death without others experiencing it, too. But for an individual to have social vitality, others must have it' (Card, 2010, p. 262). This implies that unless the social context supports our social vitality it will be compromised.

Although genocide is aimed at groups, it also operates on a very personal level because'[s] ocial death can aggravate physical death by making it indecent, removing all respectful and caring ritual, social connections, and social contexts that can make dying bearable and make one's death meaningful' (Card, 2010, p. 262). Card gives examples of a series of dehumanising processes taking place before genocide. These include lying to victims about their own survival, making them watch torture, rape and death of their loved ones, all of which are aimed at the devastation of the still-alive person's ontological base.

Additionally, Card and Marsoobian (2007, p. 11) point out that 'genocidal acts are not always or necessarily homicidal', but achieve their intended effect by inflicting harm on the victim's social vitality. Women and men may be sterilised and children separated from their families, forced to undergo cultural assimilation in a new country. Thus cross-generational links and collective memory of the community cease to exist and any future continuity is terminated, thus providing a rationale for Card's (2010) suggestion for including the concept of social death in the UN definition of genocide.

To conclude, genocide, as theorised by Card (2010), serves to show the most extreme case of social death operating on interpersonal, community, transnational and cross-generational levels. This provides a helpful starting point in unifying and clarifying the concept, grounding it in a philosophical ethics that supports its use across a range of substantive research areas.

As previously explained, the substantive fields that use the social death concept tend to focus on those facets of social death that are *most prominent within their subject area*. However, unless their subject matter is the most extreme circumstance, by doing so they find the boundaries between social death and the 'not quite so socially dead' difficult to establish. When describing interpersonal relations, the opposite of social death is commonly understood to be a social existence, a social or meaningful/worthy life. This, juxtaposed with White's observation that the wellbeing literature lacks 'a dual focus on wellbeing and "ill-being"' (2010, p. 167), poses the question: Does social death amount to 'ill-being'?

Three characteristics of White's (2010) definition of well-being seem also to be true for social death: well-being is (1) a process that is based on relations; (2) contextual and takes into account the variability of circumstances, environments, timelines and the various cultural contexts and (3) operates on an individual as well as a community level. The extent to which White's (2010) well-being and Card's (2010) social vitality are similar is worth exploring.

Here I would argue that the *most scholars using the concept of social death actually mean profoundly compromised well-being* – more often than not, they are describing the loss of *only some* of social death's facets. On the other hand, those using social death to describe the most extreme circumstances, such as solitary confinement (Guenther, 2013) or genocide (Card, 2010), refer to the loss of *most or indeed all* of these facets. Conversely, talking of 'profoundly compromised well-being' in these most extreme cases sounds somewhat precarious, as White (2010) also recognises.

We should thus recall Card's (2010) concept of social vitality, which includes all relationships which people or groups are involved in, including educational, economic, political and cultural societal structures and which she frames as an antithesis of social death. Furthermore, Card also argues that people's *social vitality is mutual*, which was powerfully demonstrated by Guenther's (2013) critical phenomenological interrogation of solitary confinement. So, what is the difference between social vitality and well-being?

Studies of well-being argue that relationships are a vital aspect of the good life. Haller and Hadler (2006, p. 169) suggest that 'happiness and satisfaction must be understood as the outcome of an interaction process between individual characteristics and aspirations on the one side, and social relations and macrosocial structures on the other side.' Furthermore, they recognise four areas in which social relations, structures and institutions facilitate and inhabit the emergence of happiness and life satisfaction. These include: '1) basic social relations and personal networks (microsocial context I); 2) sociocultural integration (microsocial context II); 3) occupational achievements and social status (microsocial context III); 4) societal and political structures and institutions (macrosocial context)' (Haller and Hadler, 2006, p. 178). All of these, while describing the interconnections between micro- and macrostructures, are congruent not only with Card's (2010) conception of social vitality but also with the studies of social death presented in this paper. Nevertheless, both the extent and type of the losses differ within substantive academic areas and in terms of individual circumstances. It is therefore possible that some of the scholars employing the social death concept in fact mean profoundly compromised well-being. This lack of distinction over the point where ill-being becomes social death indicates that the two are conceptually and structurally similar.

White's (2010) well-being comprises *material* well-being (practical welfare and standards of living), *social* well-being (social relations and access to public goods) and *human* well-being (capabilities, attitudes to life and personal relationships). All three then have an *objective* and a *subjective* dimension and are understood as processes positioned over time within a space. This, I argue, is congruent with the concerns of social death theorists.

Moreover, White's (2010) assessment of well-being is critical for studies of genocide, as it recognises that past–present–future cross-generational, spatial and historical connections are crucial for the social vitality of individuals as well as groups. Examples of this include the use of sperm as a biological weapon in the Brana Plan for ethnic cleansing, where the Muslim community was devastated by the forced creation of a new generation. No atrocity had taken a place in terms of typical genocide – indeed rather the opposite – and consequently a 'logical glitch' ensued (Card, 2010, p. 283). However, its effect remained genocidal. Similar to this event, the devastating impact of the so-called development of New Orleans after Hurricane Katrina effectively resulted in enforced birth control of the local community and their displacement. It is best captured by the question '[w]here are the black children?' (Lovell, 2011). Despite Card's (2002, 2010) efforts, these instances cannot be legally recognised as genocide because social death has not yet been included in the UN definition of genocide.

White (2010, p. 164) encounters the core ontological question by stating that 'people become who and what they are in and through their relatedness to others'. The experiences of profound ontological deficit lived by those in solitary confinement is testament to this very claim (Guenther, 2013), while the intersubjectivity found between a contemporary performer and a long-dead composer provides testimony to the contrary (McCormick, 2015). However, '[s]ocial death is not a singular biographical condition but a relational idiom of power' (Gordon, 2011, p. 13). I suggest that it is not only about what we make of our lives, as the neoliberal view of the world would have us believe, but also about *what others let us* make of it. 'There is, in fact, a whole anthropology of "people without a future" embedded in the culture of poverty assumptions that justify mass imprisonment as poverty management' (Gordon, 2011, p. 13). Similarly, Cacho (2012) titles her book: *Social death: Racialized rightlessness and the criminalization of the unprotected*, while Biehl (2014, p. 476) speaks of 'a bureaucratically and relationally sanctioned register of social death'. This begs the question of who is likely to be on this register. Giroux's (2011, p. 597) rhetoric of *social death of the social state,* where the state fails to provide social protection to those in need, finds that:

[t]hose experiencing poverty are seen as the problem and become an easy target for mobilizing middle-class fears about not just the poor, the disabled, immigrants and others who may

depend on social services, but also the social services themselves and the policies that make them possible.

So what good, if any, would come of recognising social death as the antithesis of well-being? White's (2010, p. 167) cautious warnings about the hazards of well-being include its connotation of affluence, the ways in which it may be misinterpreted by policy-makers as well as practitioners, and the ways in which 'wellbeing is profoundly de-politicising: the issue becomes not to change the world but to change the way you feel about it'. Having social death as the antithesis of well-being would not only contribute to greater theorisation of terms on each side of the continuum but would also provide more accuracy in any description of an 'ill-being' (White, 2010). It would thereby protect the theoretical rigour of social death, so crucial to genocide scholarship.

Conclusion

From observing repeatedly occurring structural similarities and differences, I argue that social death is often used too loosely both across and within varying substantive areas of research. However, to conduct any empirical investigation invites ethical obstacles and practical challenges, so it is important to have a coherent and robust theory of what we mean by social death. Using a methodology analogous to meta-ethnography (Noblit & Hare, 1988) to compare works of a wide range of scholars using the term social death, I found three underlying concepts – loss of social identity, loss of social connectedness and losses associated with the disintegration of the body – and arrived at the conclusion that social death is a multifaceted phenomenon whose conceptual framework can nonetheless be identified. However, in order to preserve the theoretical integrity of social death it should be limited only to *the most extreme circumstances, in which the majority or all of its facets are severely compromised and/or lost*. Finally, I compare the emerging conceptual framework of social death with that of well-being (White, 2010) and suggest that social death be recognised as the antithesis of well-being.

Nevertheless, much is left to be explored regarding social death's underlying conceptual framework. More works employing the social death concept need to be examined for their conceptual frameworks, both within disciplines and across them. The empirical testing of the social death conceptual framework would be possible if conducted as a cross-disciplinary investigation from its onset but with profound ethical considerations. Recognising social death as the antithesis of well-being is open to challenge as no complete conceptual framework of social death is yet available to allow comparison with well-being. Furthermore, it would be theoretically as well as empirically helpful to establish measures that could demarcate between well-being, severally compromised well-being and social death. However, in order to achieve theoretical rigour, social death must be limited to the most extreme circumstances, recalling Sudnow's (1967) point that it would be a mistake to apply the term indiscriminately to any form of social maltreatment. Nonetheless, we should also keep in mind Gordon's (2011, p. 17) warning that social death is 'something we do that can and must be stopped'.

Acknowledgements

The author thanks the many scholars, friends, the general public and anonymous reviewers who critically challenged her thoughts during the development of this theoretical proposal and to the Centre for Death and Society for its ongoing support.

Funding

This work was supported by a Graduate School Scholarship from the University of Bath.

SOCIAL DEATH

References

Agamben, G. (1998). *Homo sacer: Sovereign power and bare life*. Stanford, CA: Stanford University Press.

Atkins, S., Lewin, S., Smith, H., Engel, M., Fretheim, A., & Volmink, J. (2008). Conducting a meta-ethnography of qualitative literature: Lessons learnt. *BMC Medical Research Methodology, 8*, 1–10.

Bauby, J.-D. (1998). *The diving-bell & the butterfly*. London: Fourth Estate Limited.

Beauboeuf-Lafontant, T. (2005). Keeping up appearances, getting fed up: The embodiment of strength among African American women. *Meridians: Feminism, Race, Transnationalism, 5*, 104–123.

Biehl, J. (2004). Life of the mind: The interface of psychopharmaceuticals, domestic economies, and social abandonment. *American Ethnologist, 31*, 475–496.

Boeije, H. (2002). A purposeful approach to the constant comparative method in the analysis of qualitative interviews. *Quality & Quantity, 36*, 391–409.

Booth, A., Papaioannou, D., & Sutton, A. (2012). *Systematic approaches to a successful literature review*. London: Sage.

Borgstrom, E. (2015). Social death in end-of-life care policy. *Contemporary Social Science, 10*(3), 272–283.

Cacho, L. M. (2012). *Social death: Racialized rightlessness and the criminalization of the unprotected*. New York, NY: University Press.

Card, C. (2002). *The atrocity paradigm: A theory of evil*. Oxford: Oxford University Press.

Card, C. (2010). *Confronting evils: Terrorism, torture, genocide*. Cambridge: Cambridge University Press.

Card, C., & Marsoobian, A. T. (2007). Genocide's aftermath: Responsibility and repair. In C. Card, & A. T. Marsoobian (Eds.), *Genocide's aftermath: Responsibility and repair* (pp. 10–26). Malden, MA: Blackwell.

Caswell, G., & O'Connor, M. (2015). Agency in the context of social death: Dying alone at home. *Contemporary Social Science, 10*(3), 249–261.

Chambre, S. M. (1984). Is volunteering a substitute for role loss in old age? An empirical test of activity theory. *The Gerontologist, 24*, 292–298.

Cumming, E., & Henry, W. E. (1961). *Growing old*. New York, NY: Basic Books.

Dageid, W., & Duckert, F. (2008). Balancing between normality and social death: Black, rural, South African women coping with HIV/AIDS. *Qualitative Health Research, 18*, 182–195.

Davies, D. J. (2002). *Death, ritual and belief: The rhetoric of funerary rites*. London: Continuum.

Durkheim, E. (1951). *Suicide: A study in sociology*. New York, NY: The Free Press.

Fram, S. M. (2013). The constant comparative analysis method outside of grounded theory. *Qualitative Report, 18*, 1–25.

Gazit, Z. (2015). (Social) death is not the end: Resisting social exclusion due to suicide. *Contemporary Social Science, 10*(3), 310–322.

Gilliard, C., & Higgs, P. (2015). Social death and the moral identity of the fourth age. *Contemporary Social Science, 10*(3), 262–271.

Giroux, H. (2011). Neoliberalism and the death of the social state: Remembering Walter Benjamin's Angel of History. *Social Identities, 17*, 587–601.

Glaser, B. G., & Strauss, A. L. (1966). *Awareness of dying*. London: Weidenfeld and Nicolson.

Goffman, E. (1961). *Asylums: Essays on the social situation of mental patients and other inmates*. London: Penguin.

Goffman, E. (1963). *Stigma: Notes on the management of spoiled identity*. London: Penguin.

Gordon, A. F. (2011). Some thoughts on haunting and futurity. *Borderlands, 10*, 1–21.

Gregory, S. W., & Lewis, J. M. (1975). Social death: Or whatever happened to Doc Daneeka? *The Pacific Sociological Review, 18*, 68–82.

Guenther, L. (2013). *Solitary confinement: Social death and its afterlives*. Minneapolis: University of Minnesota Press.

Hallam, E., Hockey, J., & Howarth, G. (1999). *Beyond the body: Death and social identity*. London: Routledge.

Haller, M., & Hadler, M. (2006). How social relations and structures can produce happiness and unhappiness: An international comparative analysis. *Social Indicators Research, 75*, 169–216.

SOCIAL DEATH

Hecht, T. (1998). *At home in the street: Street children of Northeast Brazil*. Cambridge: Cambridge University Press.

Heller, J. (1955). *Catch-22*. New York, NY: Simon and Schuster.

Hockey, J., & Draper, J. (2005). Beyond the womb and the tomb: Identity, (dis)embodiment and the life course. *Body and Society, 11*, 41–58.

Jahoda, M. L. P. F., & Zeisel, H. (1972). *Marienthal: The sociography of an unemployed community*. Trowbridge: Redwood Press. First published: 1933 as Die Arbeitslosen von Marienthal.

Jamieson, R. W. (1995). Material culture and social death: African-American burial practices. *Historical Archaeology, 29*, 39–58.

Jonsson, A. (2015). Post-mortem social death – exploring the absence of the deceased. *Contemporary Social Science, 10*(3), 284–295.

Juhl, K., & Olsen, O. E. (2006). Societal safety, archaeology and the investigation of contemporary mass graves. *Journal of Genocide Research, 8*, 411–435.

Kalish, R. A. (1968). Life and death: Dividing the indivisible. *Social Science and Medicine, 2*, 249–259.

Kellehear, A. (2007). *A social history of dying*. Cambridge: Cambridge University Press.

Klass, D., Silverman, P. R., & Nickman, S. L. (1996). *Continuing bonds: New understandings of grief*. London: Routledge.

Leshem, S., & Trafford, V. (2007). Overlooking the conceptual framework. *Innovations in Education and Teaching International, 44*, 93–105.

Lovell, A. M. (2011). Debating life after disaster: Charity hospital babies and bioscientific futures in post-Katrina New Orleans. *Medical Anthropology Quarterly, 25*, 254–277.

Mauss, M. (1979). The physical effect on the individual of the idea of death suggested by the collectivity. In R. Littlewood & S. Dein (Eds.), *Cultural psychiatry and medical anthropology: An introduction and reader* (pp. 79–96). London: Bloomsbury.

McCormick, L. (2015). The agency of dead musicians. *Contemporary Social Science, 10*(3), 323–335.

Moen, P., Erickson, M. A., & Dempster-McClain, D. (2000). Social role identities among older adults in a continuing care retirement community. *Research on Aging, 22*, 559–579.

Moss, M. S., & Moss, S. Z. (1985). Some aspects of the elderly widow (er)'s persistent tie with the deceased spouse. *OMEGA-Journal of Death and Dying, 15*, 195–206.

Mulkay, M., & Ernst, J. (1991). The changing profile of social death. *Archives Européennes De Sociologie, XXXII*, 172–172.

Noblit, G. W., & Hare, R. D. (1988). *Meta-ethnography: Synthesizing qualitative studies*. London: Sage.

Norwood, F. (2009). *The maintenance of life: Preventing social death through euthanasia talk and end-of-life care: Lessons from the Netherlands*. Durham, NC: Carolina Academic Press.

Noys, B. (2005). *The culture of death*. Oxford: Berg.

Patterson, H. O. (1982). *Slavery and social death: A comparative study*. London: Harvard University Press.

Seale, C. (1998). *Constructing death: The sociology of dying and bereavement*. Cambridge: Cambridge University Press.

Silverman, P. R. (2004). *Widow to widow: How the bereaved help one another*. Hove: Routledge.

Smith, H. (2013, June 18). Moors murderer: Killing 5 children is petty crime. *Metro*, p. 17.

Steele, C., Kidd, D. C., & Castano, E. (2015). On social death: Ostracism and the accessibility of death thoughts. *Death Studies, 39*, 19–23.

Sudnow, D. (1967). *Passing on*. Englewood Cliffs, NJ: Prentice Hall.

Sweeting, H., & Gilhooly, M. (1997). Dementia and the phenomenon of social death. *Sociology of Health & Illness, 19*, 93–117.

Sweeting, H. N., & Gilhooly, M. L. (1991). Doctor, am I dead? A review of social death in modern societies. *Omega: Journal of Death and Dying, 24*, 251–269.

Toplean, A. (2015). To resist or to embrace social death? Photographs of couples on Romanian gravestones. *Contemporary Social Science, 10*(3), 296–309.

Turner, V. W. (1967). *The forest of symbols: Aspects of Ndembu ritual*. London: Cornell University Press.

Unruh, D. R. (1983). Death and personal history: Strategies of identity preservation. *Social Problems, 30*, 340–351.

Van Gennep, A. (1960). *The rites of passage*. London: Routledge.

White, S. C. (2010). Analysing wellbeing: A framework for development practice. *Development In Practice, 20*, 158–172.

White, S. C., Gaines Jr., S. O., & Jha, S. (2014). Inner wellbeing: Concept and validation of a new approach to subjective perceptions of wellbeing—India. *Social Indicators Research, 119*, 723–746.

Agency in the context of social death: dying alone at home

Glenys Caswell and Mórna O'Connor

Sue Ryder Care Centre for the Study of Supportive, Palliative and End of Life Care, School of Health Sciences, Queen's Medical Centre, University of Nottingham, Nottingham, UK

Each year, a number of bodies are found of people who have died alone at home and whose absence from daily life has not been noticed. Media reports tend to cast either these individuals as deviant, or wider society as having abandoned them to a lonely death. This paper proposes an alternative view, one in which some individuals choose to withdraw from society and enter a period of social death prior to their biological deaths. They may then be subject to a renewed social life after death, brought about through post-death social processes. The paper begins by laying out the background to the pilot study on which it draws, before discussing some of the methodological and ethical issues involved in carrying out such research. A case study is then presented as a focus for a discussion of the possible role of agency and choice within the context of social death.

Introduction

This paper argues that a number of people who live alone make the decision to withdraw from social contact with others and thus enter a self-imposed period of social death prior to their biological deaths. In doing so, they are exhibiting agency and creating identities for themselves that are based on personal choice, in accordance with the late-modern project (Giddens, 1991). Occasionally, such life choices will result in the death of the individual taking place in circumstances where their body is not found for some considerable time, and societal responses when this occurs indicate that the life choices made by that person when alive are not considered legitimate (Bauman, 2005). There are consequences for the deceased individual who lived and died alone, in that the socially perceived illegitimacy of their life choices may result in their lives and deaths being investigated and their identities recast after death in a form of social life revival (Langer, Scourfield, & Fincham, 2008). This paper makes use of a case study, drawn from pilot research, to explore how this may occur.

The paper begins by discussing social death and how the concept is used, before going on to consider dying alone and what is already known. The situation where an individual who lived alone has died whilst alone and their body has not been found for an extended period of time will be described here as a lone death; this is for the sake of brevity and clarity of meaning. There will be a brief description of some of the methodological and ethical issues involved in conducting the research upon which the paper is based and the different sources of data used will be discussed. A case study will then be presented which highlights the issues for discussion. It will be argued that Adam Jackson,[1] who features in the case study, chose to enter a stage of social death by withdrawing from social contact with others whilst still biologically alive. After his death, however, Mr Jackson was subject to processes which revived his social life, with no input from him and without consideration to his wishes. Mr Jackson exhibited agency during his lifetime, but lost the power to exercise choice after undergoing a lone death.

Background

Social death

Social death, as the term is used in this paper, is a process or state in which an individual ceases to be an active participant in the social worlds of others, and the key feature of this conceptualisation of social death is ' … the cessation of the individual person as an active agent in others' lives' (Mulkay & Ernst, 1991, p. 178). It may be that the individual concerned has been judged as close to clinical death by medical professionals, and is then treated as if already dead by healthcare staff and sometimes also by their family and friends (Glaser & Strauss, 1965; Sudnow, 1967). It may also be the case that the person shows signs that are interpreted by others as indicating membership of a group which is deemed to be moving towards biological death (Hallam, Hockey, & Howarth, 1999). This latter group may include people with dementia, or people who appear frail and old; its constitution depends upon place, time and social context. In both these cases, the individuals who are cast as socially dead cease to be active agents in the social lives of others and are treated by others as if they are of no consequence and already dead (Mulkay & Ernst, 1991).

It is not sufficient to say that all people with dementia, or all those who appear to be frail and elderly, are also socially dead. There are many people in these groups who continue to be socially significant in the lives of others. It is the case, however, that an individual may be cast as socially dead by some people and therefore not be considered as players in their social lives, but that same individual may feature prominently in the social plans and lives of others (Mulkay & Ernst, 1991). For example, an older person with dementia may be deemed of no social consequence by some members of their family and thus be socially dead to those family members, but they may simultaneously have an active 'social presence' amongst their peers (Hallam et al., 1999, p. 45). Some individuals, therefore, move in and out of periods of social death and social life and may at times be cast as socially dead and other times as socially alive.

Linked with the notion of simultaneous social death and biological life is the idea of an ongoing social life that comes after biological death. In the immediate aftermath of a death, bereaved individuals may continue to interact with the person who has died, holding their hand, talking to and reassuring them (Hallam et al., 1999; Mulkay & Ernst, 1991). Such a social existence after biological death is not restricted to the period immediately after death; however, and for many who have been bereaved, the deceased person remains an important part of their lives and everyday considerations. Bereaved people may think about the person who has died, talk to them, ask their advice and consider their feelings over an extended period of time (Valentine, 2008). As is the case with social death that occurs prior to biological death, an ongoing social life for someone who is already dead may occur in some of their relationships but not in others. A widow, for example, may continue to keep her dead husband socially alive and maintain an ongoing bond with him, while her children may not have such a relationship with their dead father (Walter, 1999).

One important factor in these accounts of social death while the individual is biologically alive, and social life when the individual is biologically dead, is that the status is usually conferred upon the individual by other people. When this happens, it is often a case of society's younger members imposing the status on older people, implying that the older individual has no choice in the matter (Hallam et al., 1999). This paper, however, suggests that for some people, this may not be the case; for a possibly small heterogeneous group of people, the decision to enter a phase of social death is one that they make for themselves. The possibility that an individual may choose social death presupposes the existence of agency, of a social actor who is able to make independent decisions and enact them. The exercise of agency is grounded within the ' ... structures and processes of the human self, conceived of as an internal conversation ... ' (Emirbayer & Mische, 1998, p. 974); the individual has social relationships with other people and with themselves and is able to consider their options, make choices and act upon those choices.

The exercise of agency, however, does not take place in a vacuum. All individuals, including those who have little contact with others, live within a social context which influences not only the choices that they make, but also the options on which they draw when making those choices. Such influences may be in the nature of structural constraints or opportunities; for example, social class positioning at birth may provide one individual with an education which opens up a range of possibilities for success in later life, whilst for another individual, his or her social class and consequent educational opportunities may limit options for the future (Giddens, 1991). The relational context within which people live may also be a source of either opportunity or constraint (Gardiner et al., 2009). Living within a supportive network of family and friends may offer a suitable milieu for an individual to utilise opportunities, while the lack of such a network may leave another individual bereft of opportunities and aware only of constraints. People living alone are not immune to the influences of the social context within which they live, and the decisions that they make about their lives are subject to the operation of constraining and enabling factors, as are the lives of all society's members (Giddens, 1991).

For some individuals, one of the choices they make will include the decision to live alone. When this is the case, there is the possibility that they will die biologically while alone at home and their body will not be found until sometime later, representing what has been termed a kind of 'abandonment' (Seale, 1995, p. 376). This may be particularly likely for individuals who have entered a period of social death, and it may hold consequences for their status as socially living individuals after death.

Dying alone

Every year, unknown numbers of people who ordinarily live alone die alone at home and their bodies are found sometime later, undergoing what is described here as a lone death. Such deaths are in contrast to what are usually described as 'good deaths' which typically involve emotional accompaniment, a suitable physical environment, supportive care from healthcare professionals and attention to spiritual needs (for discussion of these issues, see, for example, Borbasi, Wotton, Redden, & Chapman, 2005; Cipolletta & Oprandi, 2014; Hart, Sainsbury, & Short, 1998; Masson, 2002). Occasionally, the period between death and the finding of the body will be months, or even years. When this occurs, it results in media interest and headlines asking questions about the nature of contemporary society and the manner in which social relationships have changed.[2] In most cases, however, the period between the individual dying and their body being found is likely to be short, and a matter of hours or days is unlikely to cause even a ripple beyond the environs in which the death took place. The numbers of people living alone are increasing in countries such as the United Kingdom (UK) and the USA (Jamieson & Simpson, 2013; Klinenberg, 2012). In 2014, there were 7.6 million people living in single-person households in the UK (Office for National Statistics, 2015). There are 11 million people aged 65 and over in the UK, of whom 3.8 million, or 36%, live alone. Of this older group, survey findings suggest that 49% rely on the television or pets as their main form of social contact, and that 11% have less than monthly contact with other people in the form of family, friends or neighbours (Age UK, 2015).

Approximately 90% of UK deaths are of people aged over 65 (Age UK, 2015); therefore, deaths alone at home are most likely to occur amongst this age group.[3] There is little research evidence regarding the views of people living alone about how and where they would wish to die. Survey evidence suggests that between 40% and 50% of people who are terminally ill and who live alone may prefer to die at home (Aoun & Skett, 2013), but understanding the views of individuals who live alone is not straightforward, as they may be influenced by a variety of factors. Such influences may include the belief that they are not allowed to stay at home as they are dying, they may have concerns about the quality of care available and about professionals entering the private space of their home, and they may also experience a fear of dying suddenly and alone (Gott, Seymour, Bellamy, Clark, & Ahmedzai, 2004; Lloyd-Williams, Kennedy, Sixsmith, & Sixsmith, 2007).

Some individuals living alone may choose to remain alone despite the risk of a lone death, while others may not care one way or the other (Howse, 1997; Kellehear, 2009). Although lone deaths have been described in terms redolent of a lack of social contact, there is little evidence as to whether those who live alone prior to their deaths undergo a period of social death. Howse, in his study of the coroner records of 647 lone deaths of older people in Southwark and Waltham, used the terms isolation, loneliness and abandonment in his report, while acknowledging that there may be an element of choice in an individual's being alone as they approach death (Howse, 1997, pp. 24, 43–46). An earlier study categorised the individuals who underwent a lone death as reclusive, reserved, independent or sociable and came to the conclusion that while such deaths may have been contrary to expectations in the 1960s and 1970s, for some older people, living and dying alone may have been a valid choice (Bradshaw, Clifton, & Kennedy, 1978, pp. 15, 23–24).

The research evidence is therefore not vast, but suggests that some individuals who live alone make an active decision to stay at home alone as they are dying and that their lone deaths may be the result of their exercise of 'agency, resistance and dissent' (Kellehear, 2009, p. 5). It is also possible that some people who live alone may choose to withdraw from social contact and impose upon themselves a form of social death, prior to their biological deaths. The paper will now turn to a consideration of the research upon which it draws.

The research

Methodological choices

The case study on which this paper draws comes from a pilot study which aims to explore the phenomenon of lone deaths and to tease out the most appropriate ways in which this subject can be researched. Two approaches have been used. One is to recruit individuals who live alone and to explore with them their views on how they would wish to be cared for – if they wish to access care services – as they approach the end of their lives, and their views on the possibility of dying alone. The second approach has been to test the sociological autopsy as a methodology for retrospectively exploring the phenomenon of dying alone at home. This latter phase of the study is drawn upon here. It involved examining deaths which had already occurred using coroner records as a starting point, in an effort to gain some understanding of the social circumstances in which the individual lived, and then died, alone.

This methodological choice was inspired by suicide research which made an ethnographic study of coroner case files. The ethnographic approach to the study of documents required consideration of 'documents as objects of study' whilst simultaneously using the coroner files to study cases of suicide (Langer et al., 2008, p. 295). The classification of a death as suicide in England and Wales is made after an investigation and an inquest, held under the authority of the coroner, making the coroner files a logical starting point for exploring suicide. The researchers examined 100 coroner case files, which they discovered to contain a variety of artefacts, including the coroner's certificate, medical and autopsy reports, witness statements, suicide notes, police reports and photographs (Langer et al., 2008). It was not clear how useful such records would be as a way to begin the investigation of lone deaths. The office of coroner in England and Wales is a unique one. The post holder may be either medically or legally qualified[4] and the role involves conducting an investigation into sudden, suspicious or unexplained deaths in order to establish the cause of death, the identity of the deceased person and whether the death was from natural or unnatural causes. The coroner has the power to order a post-mortem examination and the authority to hold an inquest, which is a public hearing to investigate the circumstances of a particular death (Dorries, 2004).

For this study, there were issues to resolve about how to identify individuals who had lived and died alone at home. Although place of death is recorded, whether or not a person died alone at home is not a category for which statistics are generated, either for the Coroners' Service or for the Office for National Statistics,[5] unlike cause of death or the decisional outcome of an inquest. In addition, researchers do not have automatic access to coroner records unlike those, such as relatives of the deceased, who are deemed to be 'properly interested persons' (Dorries, 2004, pp. 304, 307). Furthermore, coroners are independent judicial officers who are appointed by local authorities, so that each coroner will decide for him or herself whether or not access should be given to a researcher (Coroners' Society of England and Wales, n.d., a). Access is reported as more likely to be given to researchers who can provide names and dates of death (Coroners' Society of England and Wales, n.d., b), so there was a need to pre-identify individuals of interest to the research before approaching the appropriate coroner's office.

Ethical considerations

Conducting research that involves human participants brings with it ethical issues that need to be addressed, and research about topics that are viewed as sensitive, such as dying and death, presents extra challenges (Lee, 1993). In setting up this study, there was a particular concern about involving people who had died before the research began and the impossibility of their having any choice about participation. There are differing philosophical perspectives as to whether or not those who are dead can be harmed (Tomasini, 2008; Wilkinson, 2002; Wisnewski, 2009), and it is unlikely that any of the deceased individuals who are of interest to the research will have anyone to speak for them. Researchers dealt with this dilemma by changing the names of the individuals and their locations in order to protect their anonymity. However, researchers are aware that this is a compromise and that involving those individuals who have undergone lone deaths in the research risks rewriting their identities as social beings post-death in ways that the individual may not have found acceptable. This will be discussed further below.

Data generation

A case-study approach was selected as the most appropriate way to generate and present in-depth data, and four cases from three different coroner offices were included in the pilot. The desire was to explore individual cases of lone deaths, comparing and contrasting in an effort to understand both similarities and differences (Yin, 2009). Data are presented here from one case study, selected for the variety of data sources upon which it is based and the differences in their approach to the case. The case study is that of Adam Jackson, and the data drawn upon about his life and death come from three different sources: the coroner record about his death, reports in the local press about his death and the inquest, and a research interview with Oliver, a work colleague of Adam Jackson's. These data sources differ from each other. Two are documentary, written for purposes other than research and in different contexts (Prior, 2003). The third data source was an interview in which Oliver shared with the interviewer his memories, perceptions and interpretations of Mr Jackson's beliefs and behaviour.

Coroner records proved to be a rich starting point for data on lone deaths. The coroner's record of the inquiry and the inquest into the death of Adam Jackson were focused on the fact that there had been an unexplained death, that the identity of the person who had died needed to be established and that the cause of death needed to be ascertained. In going about its legally constituted business, the coroner's office created a narrative about the dying of Adam Jackson, using specially crafted documents such as police reports, witness statements, a post-mortem report, a GP letter and the coroner's verdict. The language used by the coroner is measured, medical and technical; it is not intended to be emotional and it is produced as an account of the facts which are interpreted in a scientific manner (Langer et al., 2008; Prior, 1989).

The media coverage of the death of Adam Jackson was written from a different perspective and with a different purpose from that of the coroner record. The role of the news media is to discover fresh information that is of interest to the public, and to convey it to them as quickly and accurately as possible; at its best, the reporting of such news will be balanced and honest. There are, however, many other considerations in what is constituted as news and how it is presented (Cole & Harcup, 2009). Adam Jackson's death was reported in the newspaper covering the locality in which he lived. The coverage was largely focused on reporting the inquest and the views of people who had reason to be interested in the local area. If the report of the inquest is excluded, the views of 14 individuals were reported in the press, but only two had known Adam Jackson when he was alive. Unlike the language in the coroner record, the language used in the press was emotive and designed to prompt a reaction, thus helping to shape the opinions of those who read the stories about lone deaths in general and the death of Adam Jackson in particular (Tuchman, 1978).

Each data source used in this case study required cautious handling during analysis. None offers direct access to Adam Jackson, his life and actions, but instead each source offers an interpretation borne out of a particular purpose and context. In consequence, the case study presented below suggests an approach to life that may have been taken by Adam Jackson, drawing on all three data sources.

Case study: Adam Jackson

Adam Jackson was born in the mid-1940s in a medium-sized English city. He was an only child and his parents owned the house in which the family lived; Adam himself never married nor did he have children. His father was a self-employed carpenter and when Adam left school, he went to work for his father. After his father died in 1972, Adam and his mother continued to live in the same house, but Adam worked for a firm of builders in the city. Adam's mother died in the early 1990s, and soon after that, he retired from work when he was in his late 40s.

Adam Jackson continued to live in the family home. An ex-colleague, John, who gave evidence at the inquest, described Adam as 'a little strange, not in a frightening way, but in an autistic-type way'. John gave evidence that after Adam retired, 'I didn't have much contact with him. I just used to see him in the street … once or twice a year.' The last time John saw Adam was, he thought, during the winter of 2009–2010 when he had seen him in the queue at the bank.

SOCIAL DEATH

Another ex-colleague, Oliver, was interviewed as part of the research project. He agreed that Adam Jackson was different, but thought that he had neither autistic tendencies nor any form of mental illness:

> I don't think he had mental illness, I think it was just the demeanour that he had. I mean if you want to define being … a recluse as being a mental illness then yes he did. But if you don't, then he didn't … he wasn't normal, but he wasn't so abnormal.

Adam kept up to date with the news and was able to converse on most topics, but he rarely started a conversation. Oliver said that he and his colleagues:

> All knew he (Adam) was a private bloke … like the shutters went down with him. You could have a conversation, he was quite well read and he was up to date with current affairs … he was just a regular bloke … he was a hard worker, worked well with other people and on his own.

Adam Jackson retired after the death of his mother, but Oliver was unsure whether this was because he no longer needed the income that work provided or because it had been Adam's mother who insisted he went out to work. As far as Oliver was aware, Adam only knew about half a dozen people, from the time when he had worked in the construction firm. Although Oliver and some other colleagues predicted the end that Adam might come to, they knew that he would not have liked them visiting him just to keep an eye on him, so they did not do so. Oliver said:

> we worried at the time whether this would be his end … because so few people knew (him), I don't think he'd got a telephone or mobile, he never had visitors, we never went round to his house, you'd see him shopping in town now and again, but the thought was if anything happens to him, nobody's going to know. Nobody's going to miss him, when you do see him, it's oh, there's Adam not, where's Adam?

In Oliver's view, it was not the case that society had forgotten Adam Jackson, but rather that Adam Jackson had removed himself from society. Oliver said:

> He was happy living on his own. When you saw him in town it was just a nod … any more would have been an intrusion … he was just a nice guy who wanted to be left alone … he just blended into the background, that was the life he led and ultimately the death that he had.

Insofar as the manner of his death was concerned, Oliver felt that Adam would not have been worried about it, and Oliver believed that it was an achievement on Adam's part that he could live his life in the manner he chose for himself:

> It's not shocking that he died alone and wasn't found for four years, because he lived alone for 20 years before that and wasn't noticed … I think he died alone, but he wasn't lonely … I actually think it's a little bit of a triumph for the individual against the system … Adam lived for almost 70 years and in that time managed to keep off loads and loads of databases to the point where you can die and not be missed for four years … it's nice that if somebody wants to do that they can still do it in the twenty-first century … he just lived a very quiet, very simple personal life and I think for the vast majority of it he was happy … I think it's a credit to him that he's been able to do that.

Adam Jackson's dead body was found in his home in the spring of 2014 when a bailiff attended the house because of unpaid bills. His body was largely skeletonised, with no internal organs remaining, and the pathologist who carried out the post-mortem on behalf of the coroner presumed that the body was that of Adam Jackson. The pathologist concluded that 'no cause of death can be given' as decomposition was too advanced. As Adam Jackson had not visited his general practitioner since 2003, it was not known whether he had any medical condition that might have contributed to his death.

The police investigation found no one living nearby who knew Adam Jackson. His home was in a short terrace of houses, but the property on one side was empty and the house on the other side was occupied by several short-term tenants. The house was secure when Mr Jackson was found and there were no signs of a struggle. The police report included in the coroner's file stated:

> The property is an absolute mess ... Tons and tons of alcohol bottles strewn across the floor and no room to walk through. Loads of undisturbed cobwebs draped across doorways ... would appear no one been in the address for a very long time.

The police officer concluded that Adam Jackson 'may have been an alcoholic.' Indications in the house, from the use-by dates on food and publication dates on newspapers, suggested that Adam Jackson had been alive at the end of 2010. The coroner recorded an open conclusion when the inquest was closed in November 2014, as there was insufficient evidence to assign a cause of death (Dorries, 2004).

In the spring of 2014, the coroner issued a cremation certificate, permitting the registration of the death and the disposal of the body. As the police had been unable to find any relatives, the local authority organised the funeral, using a local firm of funeral directors. At a later date, council workers emptied the house of Adam Jackson's belongings, clearing away the last signs of his life and death.

Local media coverage of Adam Jackson's death was mainly focused on the period subsequent to the inquest. Mr Jackson was described as 'forgotten', his death a 'sad sign of our times' and 'a sad example of modern society'. His story was 'tragic' and the question was asked as to whether his death was 'a sad indictment of society today?' Adam Jackson's home and the surrounding area were described in graphic detail, setting the scene for readers of an area with a transient population and derelict buildings in the midst of which Adam Jackson lived in a house with dirty windows and closed curtains. There were photographs of the house included in the coverage, appearing unkempt and semi-derelict, but there were no pictures of Adam Jackson himself. The newspaper reporter spoke to local councillors, representatives of an organisation that works with older people and the Member of Parliament for the constituency, plus local traders and people who lived in the vicinity. Their reported comments all focused on Adam Jackson as a victim who had no control over the circumstances of his life and death and for whom readers should feel sad and perhaps a little guilty.

Oliver, however, felt that the coverage of Adam Jackson's life and death in the local press was unfair, because:

> What seemed to be missed in the papers was that although he'd been dead four years when he was found, he'd been alive for 60 odd before that and functioned quite well. He'd had a job, he'd made his own decisions and he'd managed his life ... between leaving (the firm) and dying he bothered nobody, nobody bothered him.

Discussion

Data generated in the course of research do not give direct access to reality, and must always be handled with caution (Hughes & Sharrock, 1997). In this case, we do not have access to Adam

Jackson's own thoughts and perspective, and have no way of assessing the influence that the death of his mother may have had on his decision-making processes, or how a possible problem with alcohol may have affected his life. As already noted, the data sources on which the paper does draw must be handled with care. The Coroner's record and the newspaper reports were written for specific purposes, and Oliver may have been concerned to maintain his 'moral reputation' in his evaluation of Adam Jackson's life and death (Seale, 1995, p. 376).

Choosing social death

Inquest evidence given by John and research interview data generated from Oliver suggest that Adam Jackson chose to retire when he did and from that point on, he had little contact with other people. Oliver further suggests that Adam lived the life of his own choosing, making the decision to withdraw from society so that rather than society forgetting about Adam Jackson he was the one who elected to forgo society. It certainly appears that Adam Jackson went out into the city in which he lived, for example, newspapers were brought into the house, which do not appear to have been delivered by a newsagent, and groceries were found in the house which must have been purchased. However, it also seems to be the case that he was not noticed. In the summary of the case, the coroner noted that 'he had not been seen alive for many years', but a more accurate rendering of the situation may be that Adam Jackson went out in order to supply his needs but in doing so was not noticed by other people; as Oliver expressed it, 'he just blended into the background'. This is suggestive, although by no means conclusive, of Adam Jackson deciding to withdraw from social contacts in the period preceding his biological death and thus entering a state of social death in which he impinged on the social life of no one else (Mulkay & Ernst, 1991). As an active agent, it appears likely that Adam Jackson chose social death.

Choosing social death resulted in Adam Jackson living, and then dying, in a situation which is not accepted as legitimate by the society of which he was part. Such a death is often interpreted as a failure on the part of society, of relatives, of neighbours and friends, and it presents a picture of a lonely older person who has been abandoned and rejected by other people (Kellehear, 2009; Seale, 1995). Such an interpretation negates the individual's agency and the power they held to make their own decisions, casting them as victims of life and loneliness; but it is not the case that all those who are alone are necessarily lonely (Kellehear, 2009). The media coverage of Adam Jackson's death portrayed exactly such a lonely life and death, as an older person whom society forgot. Considering the broader set of evidence, however, it appears that Mr Jackson may have been one of the individuals to whom Kellehear refers when he describes those who choose to live and die alone as a means of exercising 'agency, resistance and dissent' (Kellehear, 2009, p. 5).

Rejuvenated social life after death

When an individual chooses social death above social life whilst still biologically alive, there are a number of possible consequences that come with this decision. In the case of Adam Jackson, these consequences came into being after he had died and once his body was found. The late-modern project offers individuals the opportunity to create their own identities, choosing who they wish to be from a range of bespoke options. There are limitations to the identities that an individual can take on, and these limitations are frequently linked to social and economic positioning within a social setting (Giddens, 1991). A social setting which prizes individual identity creation may be expected to appreciate unusual identities and those who are eccentric, but this is not necessarily the case. Eccentricity and difference require to be retained within certain boundaries in order to be understood and appreciated, so that individuals experience the pressure to be simultaneously both different and ordinary (Bauman, 2005).

Adam Jackson chose to be different in a way which is not accepted as legitimate by the society within which he lived. After he died, there were legal and social processes put into practice which endeavoured to rewrite his identity in ways which would make him comprehensible to wider society. This process began once his body was found and his death had been reported to the coroner. The job of the coroner and their team was to discover who had died, when and how the death had taken place and whether there were any suspicious circumstances to the death. Once these questions were answered, the death could be certificated and registered and Adam Jackson could be entered into the statistics, as gathered by the Office for National Statistics. In this, however, Mr Jackson largely defeated the system. The pathologist was unable, because of the advanced state of decomposition, to assign a definitive cause of death and was also unable to say when death had occurred. Adam Jackson had never been arrested by the police so neither his fingerprints nor his DNA[6] were on record for comparisons to be made, and in addition his teeth were in good condition so that he had never attended a dentist and it was not possible to compare his dental records with those of the dead body.

The coroner wrote that, 'The house was secure when he was found and there was no evidence of any third party involvement, nor evidence that he had taken his own life.' The coroner and the police officers who carried out the investigation were satisfied that the dead man was Adam Jackson, but could not categorically state this to be the case; it was presumed rather than known. At the end of the inquest, the coroner reached an open conclusion which is the appropriate response when the evidence available 'does not fully or further disclose the means whereby the cause of death arose' (Dorries, 2004, p. 272). The coroner failed to find a good fit between Adam Jackson's life and death, and the categories into which those who die in England and Wales are supposed to be placed. The death of Adam Jackson is therefore cast as an open conclusion, the repository for those whose deaths do not fit into neat classifications.

The media were less circumspect in the way they treated Adam Jackson after his death. There appeared to be no question that the body was that of Adam Jackson, and the reports showed no hesitation in rewriting his identity from that of an individual who made unusual choices in his life to an individual who had no control over his life and death. This rewritten Adam Jackson was portrayed as a victim of tragic circumstance who had been abandoned by society. He had been a reclusive drinker who had preserved his mother's bedroom, as it had been when she died during the 1990s, with the implication that he had struggled and been unable to cope on his own. Such a media construction of someone who has died alone is not unusual, making moral judgements on those involved in a particular case and identifying the deceased person as having character flaws which contributed to them dying alone in a way that is constructed as undesirable. In this way, the writer of such a piece can ' … position themselves as bearers of moral messages and guardians of the community, aligned with official morality about how such a society ought to behave' (Seale, 2004, p. 973).

What the coroner record and the media coverage have also accomplished in the case of Adam Jackson is to create new social identities for him beyond his death. The coroner has established an identity for him as someone whose death was unexplained and therefore subject to inquiry. In the act of conducting this inquiry and holding an inquest, Adam Jackson has been brought into the public eye and has been subjected to what appears to have been against the wishes of the living man, that is, he has been noticed by other people. The media coverage has created an identity for Adam Jackson as a sad, tragic, lonely man who was abandoned by society and who could not cope with life without alcohol (Langer et al., 2008). Thus, the late-modern project of identity creation has been turned against a man who in life built himself an identity based on agency and independence, and it has been used to re-create an identity for Adam Jackson after his death, in an effort to make him socially understandable and acceptable (Bauman, 2005; Giddens, 1991).

The research into which Adam Jackson has been drawn without his permission is also not without responsibility in causing him to have a social life after his death. Reading, thinking and writing about him, as well as talking to Oliver about him during interview have all contributed to processes whereby the memory of Mr Jackson continues. While there is no reason to assume that we know what he would have thought of this, the man described by Oliver would have been unlikely to come forward voluntarily to participate in research. Of his inclusion in research, Oliver said:

> I don't think he'd have appreciated the press coverage because it throws him into the limelight that he really didn't want, but just discussing and sort of, I don't know, we're sort of validating his existence. I don't think he wouldn't have appreciated that … I don't think he'd have minded, although I don't think he'd have volunteered … his backstory is worth recording, it's important, but it's not the tragedy that the papers made it out to be … if he was alive now nobody still would have heard of him.

Conclusion

Evidence suggests that Adam Jackson may have chosen social death for himself while he was still alive, but that social life was chosen for him after his death by the processes that are an integral part of the English social and legal fabric. As an active social agent, Adam Jackson created his own identity, but he did so in a form that was not recognised within the social setting in which he lived. Adam Jackson was one man, and it is unknown how many others may be in a similar position to that which he occupied, opting for a form of social withdrawal and death whilst living, rather than having it imposed upon them. The pilot study upon which this paper draws was designed to test the most appropriate way in which to explore the phenomenon of the lone death. Findings suggest that coroners' case files make a good starting point offering, as they do, the possibility of further avenues of exploration beyond the documents contained in the file. Adam Jackson's story highlights a need to search for greater understanding and for differentiating between those who yearn for company as they are living and dying and those who prefer to be alone. However, his story is suggestive rather than conclusive, and the expansion of the research to encompass an examination of other lone deaths would help to promote the understanding that for some individuals living and dying entirely alone is a legitimate choice.

Individuals such as Adam Jackson eschew health and social care services, perhaps from a perception that engagement with services will bring a level of unwanted intrusion, or a forced move from home (Gott et al., 2004). Greater appreciation of the legitimacy of individuals' choices could inform the development of services that are appropriate to their needs and wishes. The British ideal 'good death', as reflected in end-of-life care policy, occurs at home, but to die alone is 'bad', even though many lone deaths are likely to be at home. Rather than being a contradiction in ideals, this paper suggests that, in some cases, the two are compatible; for some, dying alone at home may be acceptable.

Disclosure statement

Neither author will receive any financial interest or benefit arising from the direct applications of the research.

Funding

This work was supported by the British Academy [grant number SG131760].

SOCIAL DEATH

Notes

1. The names Adam Jackson, Oliver and John, which are used in this paper, are pseudonyms. Small details about Adam Jackson have also been changed in order to protect his anonymity, whilst not affecting the analytical significance of the data presented.
2. See, for example, http://www.dailymail.co.uk/news/article-1197314/Woman-85-lay-dead-flat-years-noticed-missing.html or Coroner's concern at increase in 'old and alone' deaths: http://www.bbc.co.uk/news/uk-wales-11526737
3. Such deaths are not exclusive to older people. See, for example, the case of Joyce Carol Vincent who was 38 when she died alone and whose body was not found for three years: http://www.theguardian.com/film/2011/oct/09/joyce-vincent-death-mystery-documentary
4. There are changes underway under the Coroner and Justice Act 2009, and information about this can be found on the Coroners' Society of England and Wales website here: http://www.coronersociety.org.uk/becoming_a_coroner
5. The Office for National Statistics, or ONS, is the body which produces official statistics for the UK on the economy, population and society: http://www.ons.gov.uk/ons/about-ons/index.html
6. Deoxyribonucleic acid (DNA), genetic material that makes each species and individual within the species unique. Often used in criminal investigation to identify perpetrators: https://www.gov.uk/government/uploads/system/uploads/attachment_data/file/252885/NDNAD_Annual_Report_2012-13.pdf

References

Age UK. (2015). *Later life in the United Kingdom. February 2015*. Retrieved from http://www.ageuk.org.uk/Documents/EN-GB/Factsheets/Later_Life_UK_factsheet.pdf?dtrk=true

Aoun, S. M., & Skett, K. (2013). A longitudinal study of end-of-life preferences of terminally-ill people who live alone. *Health and Social Care in the Community, 21*, 530–535.

Bauman, Z. (2005). *Liquid life*. Cambridge: Polity Press.

Borbasi, S., Wotton, K., Redden, M., & Chapman, Y. (2005). Letting go: A qualitative study of acute care and community nurses' perceptions of a 'good' versus a 'bad' death'. *Australian Critical Care, 18*(3), 104–113.

Bradshaw, J., Clifton, M., & Kennedy, J. (1978). *Found dead: A study of old people found dead*. London: Age Concern.

Cipolletta, S., & Oprandi, N. (2014). What is a good death? Health care professionals' narrations on end-of-life care. *Death Studies, 38*, 20–27.

Cole, P., & Harcup, T. (2009). *Newspaper journalism*. London: Sage.

Coroner's Society of England and Wales. (n.d., a). *Ministry of Justice*. Retrieved from http://www.coronersociety.org.uk/ministry_of_justice

Coroner's Society of England and Wales. (n.d., b). *Research*. Retrieved from http://www.coronersociety.org.uk/research

Dorries, C. (2004). *Coroners' courts: A guide to law and practice* (2nd ed.). Oxford: Oxford University Press.

Emirbayer, M., & Mische, A. (1998). What is agency? *The American Journal of Sociology, 103*, 962–1023.

Gardiner, J., Stuart, M., MacKenzie, R., Forde, C., Greenwod, I., & Perrett, R. (2009). Redundancy as a critical life event: Moving on from the Welsh steel industry through career change. *Work, Employment and Society, 23*(4), 727–745.

Giddens, A. (1991). *Modernity and self-identity*. Stanford, CA: Stanford University Press.

Glaser, B. G., & Strauss, A. L. (1965). *Awareness of dying*. London: Weidenfeld and Nicolson.

Gott, M., Seymour, J., Bellamy, G., Clark, D., & Ahmedzai, S. (2004). Older people's views about home as a place of care at the end of life. *Palliative Medicine, 18*, 460–467.

Hallam, E., Hockey, J., & Howarth, G. (1999). *Beyond the body: Death and social identity*. London: Routledge.

Hart, B., Sainsbury, P., & Short, S. (1998). Whose dying? A sociological critique of the 'good death. *Mortality, 3*(1), 65–77.

Howse, K. (1997). *Deaths of people alone*. London: Centre for Policy on Ageing and Help the Aged.

Hughes, J., & Sharrock, W. (1997). *The philosophy of social research* (3rd ed.). Harlow: Longman.

Jamieson, L., & Simpson, L. (2013). *Living alone*. Basingstoke: Palgrave Macmillan.

Kellehear, A. (2009). Dying old – and *preferably* alone? Agency, resistance and dissent at the end of life. *International Journal of Ageing and Later Life, 4*(1), 5–21.

Klinenberg, E. (2012). *Going solo*. New York, NY: The Penguin Press.

Langer, S., Scourfield, J., & Fincham, B. (2008). Documenting the quick and the dead: A study of suicide case files in a coroner's office. *The Sociological Review, 56*, 293–308.

Lee, R. M. (1993). *Doing research on sensitive topics*. London: Sage.

Lloyd-Williams, L., Kennedy, V., Sixsmith, A., & Sixsmith, J. (2007). Perceptions of people over the age of 80 on issues surrounding death and dying. *Journal of Pain and Symptom Management, 34*, 60–66.

Masson, J. D. (2002). Non-professional perceptions of 'good death': A study of the views of hospice care patients and relatives of deceased hospice care patients. *Mortality, 7*(2), 191–209.

Mulkay, M., & Ernst, J. (1991). The changing profile of social death. *European Journal of Sociology, 32*, 172–196. doi:10.1017/S0003975600006214

Office for National Statistics. (2015). *Family and households, 2014*. Retrieved from http://www.ons.gov.uk/ ons/rel/family-demography/families-and-households/2014/families-and-households-in-the-uk–2014. html

Prior, L. (1989). *The social organization of death*. Basingstoke: Macmillan.

Prior, L. (2003). *Using documents in social research*. London: Sage.

Seale, C. (1995). Dying alone. *Sociology of Health & Illness, 17*, 376–392.

Seale, C. (2004). Media constructions of dying alone: A form of 'bad death'. *Social Science & Medicine, 58*, 967–974.

Sudnow, D. (1967). *Passing on The social organization of dying*. Upper Saddle River, NJ: Prentice-Hall.

Tomasini, F. (2008). Research on the recently dead: An historical and ethical examination. *British Medical Bulletin, 85*, 7–16.

Tuchman, G. (1978). *Making news: A study in the construction of reality*. New York, NY: The Free Press.

Valentine, C. (2008). *Bereavement narratives*. Abingdon: Routledge.

Walter, T. (1999). *On bereavement the culture of grief*. Maidenhead: Open University Press.

Wilkinson, T. M. (2002). Last rights: The ethics of research on the dead. *Journal of Applied Philosophy, 19*, 31–41.

Wisnewski, J. J. (2009). What we owe the dead. *Journal of Applied Philosophy, 26*, 54–70.

Yin, R. K. (2009). *Case study research* (4th ed.). Thousand Oaks, CA: Sage.

Social death and the moral identity of the fourth age

Chris Gilleard and Paul Higgs

UCL Division of Psychiatry, Faculty of Brain Sciences, University College London, London, UK

The bleaker aspects of old age have been encapsulated in the concept of a fourth age which has been likened to a metaphorical 'black hole' where human agency is no longer visible. This paper explores what such a formulation might mean for the moral standing of mentally and physically infirm persons. Does the idea of a fourth age reinforce representations of dementia as a form of social death or does the status of those defined by the moral imperative of care benefit from the narratives and practices of their carers who keep socially alive such persons whatever their degree of dementia? This paper argues that those persons at risk of being enveloped by the fourth age are not inherently deprived of a social life even if it is a social life that their previous self would not have chosen. The moral imperative of care forms a key part element of the fourth age – for both good and ill. Recognising the role of carers in realising or rejecting the fourth age imaginary means also valuing their agency.

Introduction

In a paper published in the *Lancet* in 2010, Daniel George wrote: 'The everyday language we use to describe dementia shapes our perceptions of brain ageing and even contributes to what has been called the "social death" of those most severely affected' (2010, p. 586). He goes on to argue that not only does the language used about dementia 'guide feelings of enmity and fear', but it also leads to dementia being seen 'as something external of us'. In identifying the contribution of language to the construction of the social death of people with dementia, George helps situate the concerns of this paper which are to consider the nature of the social identity attributed to mentally frail old people, what we have termed the 'social imaginary' of the fourth age. In particular, we are interested in examining whether the fourth age, conceived in this way, necessarily condemns people to 'social death' and therefore places them outside of social relations (Higgs & Gilleard, 2015). This question is important because the idea of the social death of the person with dementia is one which is increasingly rejected in most contemporary accounts of the social relations surrounding dementia in favour of positions supporting the continuing role of 'personhood' (Dewing, 2008; Kitwood, 1997). For those advocating a personhood approach, the difficulty with the concept of social death is that it implies the loss of personhood while the individual with dementia is alive and therefore deprives him or her of their 'human rights'.

However, if the fourth age is thought of as 'ageing without agency' (Gilleard & Higgs, 2010), the challenge for people with dementia is less about their personhood going unrecognised as their various dependencies that position them under the agency of others through the 'imperative of care'. Once activated this imperative of care provides (for good or for ill) a necessary scaffolding potentially preventing the social death of the person with dementia while potentially foreclosing other aspects of personhood. The social imaginary of the fourth age may keep alive the identity of the person with dementia, but it also serves to frame the individual as a non-agentic object of concern even while maintaining the individual in the complex pattern of social and cultural relations that constitutes caring.

These arguments might seem to run contrary to much discussion about dementia and personhood. To expound our argument, we need to start by defining our terms. This we do in the first part of this paper, by explicating the concepts of 'the fourth age', 'moral identity' and 'social death'. In the second half of the paper, we address the various possible relationships between these terms. We conclude by arguing that mentally frail old people can be maintained as socially alive persons, even as their care is carried out under the aegis of the fourth age, and despite being considered as having a limited or even lost agency.

The fourth age

The concept of 'the fourth age' was introduced into modern gerontology by Peter Laslett, in his book *A Fresh Map of Life* (Laslett, 1989, 1996). Laslett described the fourth age as a period of dependency and decrepitude, which he contrasted with the autonomy and achievement in later life that he attributed to the third age when the responsibilities of work and family were shed and opportunities for self-fulfilment beckoned (Laslett, 1996, p. 192). While Laslett saw the fourth age as a final stage of life normally occurring after the third age had been attained, he acknowledged that for some illness may cause a rapid fall into the fourth age, with no opportunity for any third age, while for others death may come so swiftly it pre-empts the possibility of a fourth age.

Paul Baltes took up the theme of the fourth age which he located as a distinct chronological period associated with the age of the oldest old, typically after the age of 80 (Baltes & Smith, 2003). He likened the division between the third and fourth age to the American psychologist Neugarten's earlier distinction between the 'young' old (60–74) and the 'old' old (75+) (1974). But for Baltes, this divide represented more than a matter of mere chronology. For him, there was a significant *qualitative* distinction between the empirically realisable possibilities of the third age and the intractability of loss that characterised the fourth (Baltes, 2006). Baltes' conceptualisation of the fourth age resonated with the earlier idea of 'terminal decline' which argued for a distinction between the positive growth of years lived since birth and the deterioration taking place in the years leading up to death (Palmore & Cleveland, 1976).

In our own work we have provided an alternative approach to the fourth age which differs markedly in its point of reference. Based neither on any fixed bio-chronology nor on individual stages of life, we proposed that the fourth age is a social imaginary (Gilleard & Higgs, 2010; Higgs & Gilleard, 2015). We draw the term 'social imaginary' from the work of the French theorist Cornelius Castoriadis in his *The Imaginary Institution of Society* to refer to the way that society and its institutions are given meaning by its members (1987). For Castoriadis, the function of 'social imaginaries' is to give meaning to modern society's unstructured and inarticulate sense of the world (Castoriadis, 1987, p. 39). Social imaginaries have both a creative function – ascribing changing or inventing meanings for social institutions and practices – and an alienating aspect, when these meanings take on a life of their own, excluding or proscribing alternative meanings and interpretations (Castoriadis, 1987). For the Canadian philosopher Charles Taylor, social imaginaries provide the social cognitions supporting mutual expectancies and social trust – the sense of togetherness (2004). The role of 'public opinion' and the 'mass media' serves as important vehicles in conveying the outlines of modern social imaginaries – whether positively as in 'our team', 'our government' or 'our boys', or negatively as in 'those gypsies', 'those immigrants' or simply 'those people'.

Old age, we have suggested, has long functioned as such a social imaginary, a social position that is either loved, respected or feared; sought after or shunned; attributed power or denied it; in short, a term whose cultural meaning is open to interpretation of what it means to be 'old'. The fourth age is the dark side of this imagined old age, the repository of all the feared and disdained aspects of age and agedness. In contrast to the authority of age with its notions of maturity and/or seniority, the fourth age is associated with senility and senescence. It is not our intention here to explore all the various influences shaping its imaginary (see Higgs & Gilleard, 2015 for a fuller treatment); here we can only briefly outline what we consider to be the four key vectors making up its contemporary form before exploring in more detail one particular vector, the imperative of care and its role in defining what can be thought of as the *moral identity* of the fourth age.

Vectors of the fourth age

At the heart of the fourth age imaginary is the social construction of frailty (\Higgs & Gilleard, 2015), with its various relationships to bio-medicine, society and the moral universe. For some time bio-medical scientists have been preoccupied with identifying a syndrome of 'frailty' distinct from both age and disease, one that serves as a biomarker of biological vulnerability. Associated with this 'laboratory science' have been those practising clinicians who have sought to incorporate failures or dysfunctions in most organ systems, and in mental health and social resources, creating a bio-psycho-social omnivore that sucks up every late life falling into its maws. The objectification of frailty represented by such bio-medical endeavours is one important aspect of the fourth age. Another equally important, if rather different, vector is that of abjection.

Abjection, as used by Georges Bataille in his essay 'Abjection and miserable forms', links certain social positions with their proximity to dirt and disgust (1999). Formulated as an abject class are all those whose utter impoverishment (culturally, financially and/or socially) leads them to and keeps them attached to an inescapable life of dirty work and regular contact with what the rest of society manages to avoid or at least conceal. This concept of abjection was further developed by the French feminist writer Julia Kristeva in her book *Powers of Horror: Essays in Abjection* (1982). Much more than Bataille, Kristeva concentrated upon the intra-psychic aspects of abjection, the psychological attributions associated with abject objects and the relationship between those abject objects and their abject subject. Drawing upon both Bataille and Kristeva, abjection can be theorised as a form of social division or social status with its accompanying intra-psychic and inter-personal 'state of being'.

The abjection of the fourth age might seem to be concerned with incontinence, a lack of self-care or the seemingly purposeless behaviour of older people with dementia. All these may well serve as signifiers of people's abject circumstances, but they are rendered more 'pitifully' abject by an evident lack of agency – the individual's apparent inability to conceal his or her 'failings' whether through physical weakness, mental limitation or other factors. This combination of 'objectified frailty' and 'distanced abjection' lends itself to the process of 'othering' – that failure to acknowledge the subjective agency of an older person, which constitutes the third vector in the social imaginary of the fourth age.

Othering is essentially a catch-all term to describe the attributions made by other people of persons who seem powerless to assert their own identity or realise their social agency. As a concept, 'othering' has a long and complex history within the academy. Its systematic use in cultural studies has been to represent the process whereby identities are attributed to those who have for various reasons become subject to the power of another (Spivak, 1988). This process was first modelled on the relationship of colonial peoples to their imperial rulers, as 'subaltern subjects' who were given no voice as subjects in their own right. Denied their own subjectivity, they exist as forever third persons in forever third worlds. Spivak helped develop the academic field of 'postcolonial' studies where the narratives and practices through which particular colonial regimes 'othered' those whom they ruled over were explored. While the concept of othering was first explored within such postcolonial contexts, more recently it has been applied to health- and social-care settings to describe how staff controlling health- or social-care 'other' those subject to particular care regimes (Canales, 2000, 2010; MacCallum, 2002).

Canales has suggested that a distinction be made between practices that actively support an 'inclusionary' othering and those that adopt a more traditional 'exclusionary' othering associated with marking and naming those considered different (Canales, 2000). As she points out, 'it is through others that we come to see and define self, and it is our ability to take that role that allows us to see ourselves through others' (Canales, 2000, p. 17). She argues that the process of othering is not inherently 'bad' and that it can enable people in very different circumstances engage with each other, as 'others', without thereby oppressing or being oppressed. Accepting difference and otherness, even non-reciprocity, she suggests, can still make care possible, whether from a sense of obligation or from feelings of pity, even though care is constrained by this sense of intractable 'otherness'. Thus conceived, othering can inform even if it does not determine the moral imperative of care, the fourth vector constituting the social imaginary of the fourth age.

The imperative of care and the moral identity of the fourth age

In charting the 'social death' implied by the loss of agency embedded within the fourth age, we soon come up against the moral imperative of care. The tradition of offering charity to orphans and widows, the aged and infirm predates modernity. It forms a common theme in all the Abrahamic religions. In Europe, the Reformation and the Counter-Reformation of the sixteenth and seventeenth centuries sharpened the distinction between the deserving and undeserving poor. Previously, it has been argued that the act of giving was considered more important than the character of the recipients. Charity was a practice expected of its adherents by their religious affiliation to secure their own salvation. The secularisation of poverty associated with the Reformation lead to more attention being paid to the recipients – on who deserved 'caritas'. Subsequent developments continued to privilege the impotent poor, especially the most impotent, the aged and infirm, who were not only offered better accommodation and diet in the alms-houses, poorhouses and workhouses, but were also deemed more eligible for 'outdoor relief'.

When the machinery of the British poor law was dismantled during the first half of the twentieth century, the greatest number of people occupying 'long stay beds' – in the workhouses, the infirmaries and the various asylums – were the aged sick. They were also among the last to gain access to the new hospital regimes which had thus far excluded them (Smith, 1990). As the post-war welfare state lumbered into action, 'care of the aged' presented it with some of its greatest challenges. Though among the most deserving, the aged sick were also among the least rewarding to look after, creating a degree of ambivalence on the part of the post-war welfare state. The aged sick could not be ignored. Everyone agreed that 'something needed to be done'. But what was most often done typically took place out of sight of the collective 'us' that constituted our collectively imagined 'welfare society' and much of it was, in retrospect, inadequate, inefficient and at times uncaring (Webster, 1991).

Foremost among the challenges arising from the integration of old people into the health-care system was agreeing and organising that care – who needed it, where should it take place and how should it be funded. As always, the aged sick most often received care within the family, by individuals whose relationship to the person receiving care was that of a wife, daughter, husband, son or daughter-in-law. Caregiving responsibilities followed from the moral identities assigned within and assumed by members of the family (Finch, 1989). By the 1980s as part of the move towards 'community care', the wives, daughters, husbands, sons and daughters-in-law began to be relabelled 'carers'. Surveys were conducted exposing the plight and even the 'oppression of carers' (Dalley, 1988). The aged sick had already been relabelled 'the elderly mentally and physically infirm'; now, those who helped them were known as their 'carers'. Local authorities complained that they could no longer afford extending subsidised accommodation to those who were merely socially needy or poor; hospitals, on the other hand, were becoming uncomfortably blocked by their aged patients whose care they asserted did not 'need' the costly ministrations of hospital doctors and nurses. Care needed to be relocated within the community, and in any case, institutions were breeding grounds of an exclusionary othering. Keeping elderly mentally and physically infirm persons at home was morally and financially a better option.

Signs of an ecologically framed crisis were increasingly predicted – rising tides of dementia, tsunamis of frailty – as an apocalyptic demography of agedness was formulated out of the ageing of already ageing societies (Robertson, 1990). How could this crisis be managed if not by ever tighter targeting and ever finer distinctions of frailty? As the networks of formal care were drawn tighter, long-term care was increasingly purchased from the non-state sector as offering 'better value'. What had once been an exclusive and exclusionary service for an elite few, the clients of private home nursing and nursing homes, was now expanded into a democratic marketplace whose customers were not so much the wealthiest but the most aged sick. Would such care prevent further 'frailure'? Would it ameliorate the abjection of the frail and the isolated older person, replacing the exclusionary 'othering' of the past with an inclusionary care service for the future? Or, might it have the opposite effect – expanding the possibilities of abjection, and more profoundly othering care recipients by constructing narratives for them of person-centred, paid compassionate care, service cultures of dementia rendered incoherent by the everyday practices that were shaped not by the wishes of informed and well-off elderly customers but by the abjection and frailures of these newly designated 'clients'?

'Piss on your pity' is a slogan that has been used by mostly younger sections of the disability movement to reassert their agency in the face of 'care'. But who can speak out for those who are unaware of, or unable to politicise, their incontinence, who, conveniently packaged in old age nappies, are labelled 'doubly incontinent, change regularly'? Should we avoid feeling pity for them and insist on their status as clients engaged in an equal exchange of cash for care? Or must we wear hope with a mourning band when confronted by what Lionel Trilling has called 'the essential immitigability of the human condition' (Trilling, 1972, p. 156)? Of course we should try harder, 'fail better' in Beckett's words (2009). Might we sometimes, however, also need to accept the idea of 'social death' as itself a kind of compassionate care, treating dementia as an involuntary haven for those for whom being forever a fully human agent has become simply too hard and too painful?[1]

Social death and dementia

The concept of social death was introduced into the social sciences in the 1960s by Glaser and Strauss who observed how, in hospital, some people often seemed to die socially – as people – before they died biologically – as bodies (1966). Drawing upon their work, Mulkay and Ernst have defined social death as 'the cessation of the individual person as an active agent in other's lives', acknowledging that individuals may be dead for some parties yet socially alive for others (1991, p. 178). They identified the 'elderly' as a group particularly prone to undergoing this kind of social death, especially in the context of age-segregated nursing and residential homes and suggested that 'a basic distinction [be made] between those who are deemed to be close to death and those for whom death is not thought to be imminent' (Mulkay & Ernst, 1991, p. 183). This distinction they summarised as one between the fit and the frail, with the former serving to define more clearly the death of the latter. The ageing of later life in contemporary societies, Mulkay and Ernst concluded, meant that 'a substantial part of those extra years of biological functioning that have been acquired ... are likely to be spent ... in a condition closely approaching social death' (1991, p. 194). The parallels between Baltes and Laslett's 'third versus fourth ages' approach are clear in this formulation.

The term 'social death' was applied to people with dementia in a series of papers by Helen Sweeting. Sweeting and her colleague Mary Gilhooly outlined the process that led people with dementia to become 'socially dead' in the minds of their carers (Sweeting & Gilhooly, 1991, 1997). They drew links with, while making distinctions between, the loss of self or personhood ascribed to dementia and the idea of social death. They pointed out that some families may often remain actively involved with patients in a vegetative state, illustrating the 'example of social life in the face of loss of personhood', while others may be treated as socially dead despite the existence of personhood, such as when 'a doctor may discuss a diagnosis with other staff in the patient's presence as if they were an inanimate object' (Sweeting & Gilhooly, 1997, p. 98).

Sweeting and Gilhooly observed a variable set of statuses ascribable to people with dementia by their relatives. These they broadly classified into (a) those who were 'socially alive and treated with attributed personhood', (b) those who were 'socially alive but treated without attributed personhood' and (c) those who were 'socially dead and treated without attributed personhood'. Importantly, they found that both the loss of personhood and the idea of social death made sense to and were found meaningful to the carers themselves even if they did not necessarily apply these concepts to their family member.

How might these statuses or social positions – a loss of personhood, social death and the need to be cared for – be reconciled? Is caring an antidote to letting someone die socially, or can it also be one aspect of realising a social death? Is social death primarily a matter of not caring for a person, or of care without really caring about the person, providing disinterested and dispassionate care to mentally frail citizens whose personhood is past? Can these various concepts of social death, the imperative of care and the fourth age be (more) usefully linked?

Social death, personhood and the moral imperative of the fourth age

Since the publication of Mulkay and Ernst's paper and Sweeting and Gilhooly's work, little attention has been given to the idea of social death among older people with dementia. The early 'carer-focused' literature that spoke of dementia as the 'loss of self' (Small, Geldart, Gutman, & Clarke Scott, 1998, p. 292) has been replaced by more 'person-centred' narratives that seek to promote inclusionary practices (Brannelly, 2011). The implication is that narratives of 'loss of self' and 'social death' do not so much describe as ascribe a negative status to the person with dementia, contributing in effect to the exclusionary othering of people with dementia through a process that was described by Kitwood as 'malignant social psychology' (Kitwood, 1993, 1997; Kitwood & Bredin, 1992).

The turn from what might be deemed carer-led narratives to narratives that acknowledge and sometimes privilege the perspective of the person with dementia can be seen as a turn away from exclusionary towards inclusionary othering – a rescuing of persons from disappearing into the darkest shadows of the fourth age. Giving space to persons with dementia, respecting their wishes, supporting their identity and recognising their individuality seem crucial in preventing such individuals' depersonalisation and their social dying. The work of Tom Kitwood and his colleagues focused on developing the person with dementia's agentic potential in order to be able to act within the world. The crucial aspect of care within this person-centred philosophy was to change the cultural and social circumstances that undermine the personhood of the individual with dementia.

The focus upon the individual that is implicit in this model of dementia care has been criticised by Bartlett and O'Connor (2007), who argue that the issue of power remains unaddressed. Instead of focusing upon prioritising personhood, they advocate an approach based on the politics of citizenship. A person with dementia is entitled to the same from life as everyone else; it is their shared citizenship, not their personhood, that counts. However, as citizenship tends to assume the individual's capacity to exercise citizen rights and responsibilities, it needs further elaboration if it is to avoid the essentialism that besets ideas of personhood. Bartlett and O'Connor argue that we should not privilege any one notion of citizenship and instead see citizenship as the outcome of 'acts of power' in which people with dementia are actors co-constructing their own reality. Even person-centred care viewed through the lens of citizenship remains a form of othering, however, and has itself been subject to a degree of criticism. Behuniak (2010), for example, has pointed out that what often lies behind the person-centred approach is a position focused on the idea of the person as a legal construct. Even if these legal constructs are ascribed the status of citizens rather than persons, it does not change this point of reference. Instead she argues people with dementia should be regarded as 'vulnerable persons' who may need at times special protection or care because of diminished capacity. This, she asserts, does not strip the person of rights, dignity or citizenship because it is guided by the shared empathy that is common to us all. Such empathy leads to a compassion that is rooted in an equality between human beings and an assumption of human autonomy. These she sees as the higher forms of power which integrate rather than exclude people with dementia from society.

It is problematic, however, that this critique of person-centred approaches leaves the issue of compassion in the same situation as those criticising ideas of pity. Who decides what for whom? This leads once again to the moral imperative of care. While it might be more virtuous to see the debate in terms of the protection of rights to participate as much as possible rather than ensuring people's protection from themselves as failed agents, the social imaginary of the fourth age cannot be brushed aside simply by reconstructing the narratives of care. How people with dementia are helped to maintain their position in society is ultimately down to the efforts of others. It is not a matter of individual choice. As all the positions outlined above concur, it involves a degree of *social* intent and the necessary diffusion of power from persons with dementia towards people without it. Rather than denying this process, it is important to recognise and support it, giving due value to the person with dementia in large part by giving value to those who have to act for such persons. It may be radical, but it is not obviously restitutive to 'piss on their pity'). By showing concern for those who are concerned about – and who care for – the person with dementia one can help enable them to hold off the shadows of the fourth age for as long as they can and as long as they desire to.

Conclusion

The fourth age can be understood as a feared imaginary of old age. Much of that fear settles on the loss of agency that is associated with frailty, particularly mental frailty and the perceived abjection of an undignified journey towards non-existence. The presence and salience of such a social imaginary, we feel, help explain the widespread fear of late-life dementia reported among those reaching or already entering later life (Breining et al., 2014; Cantegreil-Kallen & Pin, 2012). Part of that fear can be represented as a fear of undergoing a premature social death – of becoming irrevocably lost to one's self as a concerned agent involved with the business of living.

SOCIAL DEATH

Alongside the abjection, frailty and loss of social agency which fashion the fourth age's imaginary, there exists a moral imperative to care that ties those in the shadows of the fourth age to the rest of the social world. Collective and familial expressions of this imperative of care have a long history across many cultures and within many religious traditions. Social death, we suggest, is unimaginable without the moral imperative to care and both can be understood as aspects of the fourth age's social imaginary. Their intimate linkage arises through the development of caregiving narratives and practices within the family and within social relationships that operate between the fit and the frail. The paradox lies in what orients the transformation of care; the perceived changes that are viewed not as change and certainly not as 'development' but as increased dependency and decreased agency.

Dementia presents an acute form of this paradox. As the updating of self begins to fail, it is increasingly what Ricoeur has called the 'sameness of self' that serves to maintain personhood (Ricoeur, 1992). With an increasing disconnection between the changes to self that others begin sooner or later to observe, the maintenance of sameness (identity) comes at a growing inter-personal cost. It becomes harder to treat the person as the same self when the person's actions, attitude and discourse bear growing witness not only to change but also to otherness. Within this conflict between self-sameness and self-change, care takes on new powers, including the power to effect or deny the social death of the person as the past self, who is deemed other to that same self.

Such a death might once have been wished for by the person affected, as a way of preventing the indignity of becoming evidently other to oneself, an indignity that the carer is helpless – as carer – to prevent. In such circumstances, pity more than compassion might seem the more appropriate, or more possible, emotional response with which to carry on caring for someone who has ceased to be the same self, who has become 'other'. Whether or not this kind of acceptance constitutes social death, or whether or not it negates some essentialised concept of 'personhood', we would argue that it does not necessarily constitute not caring even if it is caring in memory of a past self no longer seemingly present. Recognising and valuing the social being of the person being *cared for* in their past sameness and in their present difference can still be *caring about* the person with dementia – in the sense of protecting and providing for that person. However, we have argued this also requires recognising and valuing the social being of the person or persons who are doing the caring, protecting them too from the darker and depersonalising aspects of the fourth age. Sometimes that might mean choosing a social death.

Note

1. This is in essence the position recently articulated by the British actress, Sheila Hancock, in her comments on the 'selfishness' of those older people who have not planned their long-term care (Furness, *Daily Telegraph*, Wednesday, 29 April 2015).

References

Baltes, P. B. (2006). Facing our limits: Human dignity in the very old. *Daedalus, 135*(1), 32–39.

Baltes, P. B., & Smith, J. (2003). New frontiers in the future of aging: From successful aging of the young old to the dilemmas of the fourth age. *Gerontology, 49*(2), 123–135.

Bartlett, R., & O'Connor, D. (2007). From personhood to citizenship: Broadening the lens for dementia practice and research. *Journal of Aging Studies, 21*(2), 107–118.

Bataille, G. (1999). Abjection and miserable forms. (Y. Shafir, Trans.). In S. Loetinger (Ed.), *More & less* (pp. 8–13). Cambridge, MA: MIT Press.

Beckett, S. (2009). *Worstward Ho!, in Company/Ill Seen, Ill Said/Worstward Ho/Stirrings Still.* London: Faber & Faber.

Behuniak, S. M. (2010). Toward a political model of dementia: Power as compassionate care. *Journal of Aging Studies, 24*(4), 231–240.

Brannelly, T. (2011). Sustaining citizenship: People with dementia and the phenomenon of social death. *Nursing Ethics, 18*(5), 662–671.

Breining, A., Lavallart, B., Pin, S., Leon, C., Moulias, S., Arwidson, P., … Verny, M. (2014). Perception of Alzheimer's disease in the French population. *The Journal of Nutrition, Health & Aging, 18*(4), 393–399.

Canales, M. K. (2000). Othering: Toward an understanding of difference. *Advances in Nursing Science, 22* (4), 16–31.

Canales, M. K. (2010). Othering: Difference understood?: A 10-year analysis and critique of the nursing literature. *Advances in Nursing Science, 33*(1), 15–34.

Cantegreil-Kallen, I., & Pin, S. (2012). Fear of Alzheimer's disease in the French population: Impact of age and proximity to the disease. *International Psychogeriatrics, 24*(1), 108–116.

Castoriadis, C. (1987). *The imaginary institution of society.* Cambridge: Polity Press.

Dalley, G. (1988). *Ideologies of caring: Rethinking community and collectivism.* Basingstoke: Macmillan Education.

Dewing, J. (2008). Personhood and dementia: Revisiting Tom Kitwood's ideas. *International Journal of Older People Nursing, 3*(1), 3–13.

Finch, J. (1989). *Family obligations and social change.* Cambridge: Polity Press.

Furness, H. (2015, April 29). Sheila Hancock: It is stupid to avoid thinking about living in a care home. *Daily Telegraph.* Retrieved April 29, 2015, from http://www.telegraph.co.uk/news/health/elder/11569456/Sheila-Hancock-it-is-stupid-to-avoid-thinking-about-living-in-a-care-home.html

George, D. R. (2010). The art of medicine: Overcoming the social death of dementia through language. *The Lancet, 376*, 586–587.

Gilleard, C., & Higgs, P. (2010). Aging without agency: Theorizing the fourth age. *Aging & Mental Health, 14*(2), 121–128.

Glaser, B. G., & Strauss, A. L. (1966). *Awareness of dying.* New Brunswick, NJ: Transaction.

Higgs, P., & Gilleard, C. (2015). *Rethinking old age: Theorising the fourth age.* London: Palgrave Macmillan.

Kitwood, T. (1993). Towards a theory of dementia care: The interpersonal process. *Ageing and Society, 13* (1), 51–67.

Kitwood, T. (1997). *Dementia reconsidered: The person comes first.* Buckingham: Open University Press.

Kitwood, T., & Bredin, K. (1992). Towards a theory of dementia care: Personhood and well-being. *Ageing and Society, 12*(3), 269–287.

Kristeva, J. (1982). *The power of horror: An essay on abjection.* New York, NY: Columbia University Press.

Laslett, P. (1989). *A fresh map of life.* London: Weidenfeld & Nicolson.

Laslett, P. (1996). *A fresh map of life* (2nd ed.). London: Macmillan Press.

MacCallum, E. J. (2002). Othering and psychiatric nursing. *Journal of Psychiatric and Mental Health Nursing, 9*(1), 87–94.

Mulkay, M., & Ernst, J. (1991). The changing profile of social death. *European Journal of Sociology, 32*(1), 172–196.

Neugarten, B. L. (1974). Age groups in American society and the rise of the young-old. *The Annals of the American Academy of Political and Social Science, 415*(1), 187–198.

Palmore, E., & Cleveland, W. (1976). Aging, terminal decline, and terminal drop. *Journal of Gerontology, 31*(1), 76–81.

Ricoeur, P. (1992). *Oneself as another* (K. Blamey, Trans.). Chicago, IL: University of Chicago Press.

Robertson, A. (1990). The policies of Alzheimer's disease: A case study in apocalyptic demography. *International Journal of Health Services, 20*(3), 429–442.

Small, J. A., Geldart, K., Gutman, G., & Clarke Scott, M. A. (1998). The discourse of self in dementia. *Ageing and Society, 18*(3), 291–316.

Smith, F. B. (1990). *The people's health, 1830–1910*. London: Weidenfeld & Nicolson.

Spivak, G. C. (1988). Can the subaltern speak? In C. Nelson & L. Grossberg (Eds.), *Marxism and the interpretation of culture* (pp. 271–313). Basingstoke: Macmillan.

Sweeting, H., & Gilhooly, M. (1997). Dementia and the phenomenon of social death. *Sociology of Health & Illness, 19*(1), 93–117.

Sweeting, H. N., & Gilhooly, M. L. (1991). Doctor, am I dead? A review of social death in modern societies. *OMEGA – Journal of Death and Dying, 24*(4), 251–269.

Taylor, C. (2004). *Modern social imaginaries*. Durham, NC: Duke University Press.

Trilling, L. (1972). *Sincerity and authenticity*. Cambridge, MA: Harvard University Press.

Webster, C. (1991). The elderly and the early national health service. In M. Pelling & R. M. Smith (Eds.), *Life, death and the elderly in historical perspective* (pp. 138–159). London: Routledge.

Social death in end-of-life care policy

Erica Borgstrom

Health Services Research and Policy, London School of Hygiene and Tropical Medicine, London, England

> Social death denotes a loss of personhood. The concept of social death is engaged with in English end-of-life care policy that sees social death before physical death as a problem. Policy-makers posit that dying persons are likely to be subject to a social death prior to their physical death unless they play an active and aware role in planning their death, facilitated through communication and access to services. Such a view foregrounds a vision of agency and does not address Sudnow's critique of how care of the dying focuses on the body.

Introduction

The dying trajectory for most people has become prolonged due to demographic and epidemiological changes, with more people dying in older age with multi-morbidities, including dementia (Murray, Kendall, Boyd, & Sheikh, 2005). Sociological and anthropological work around ageing, dementia and dying has suggested that the asynchronous decline of bodily and cognitive functions, often attributed to these demographic and epidemiological changes, and the current care practices used to manage this decline, may result in a form of social death, whereby people are treated as if they are already or nearly dead (e.g. Froggatt, 2001). Research on social death suggests that when it occurs before physiological death (i.e. the death of the body), it marks a loss of personhood (Lawton, 2000). These experiences of 'prolonged dying', loss of personhood and the corresponding culturally constructed sensitivities around this have ignited and united public and professional interest in death (Spiro, 1996). Consequently, within England there has been a search for normalising 'good death' that controls this decline, both in terms of euthanasia and assisted dying (N. Richards, 2014), and in extending hospice and palliative care to general end-of-life care (Clark, 2002). In this article, I outline how policy-makers have engaged with different notions of social death in constructing and justifying end-of-life care policy, as they seek to address and improve the quality of care when dying and the experience of death.

End-of-life care (EOLC) seeks to systematically address the care of the dying, and the End of Life Care Strategy (Department of Health, 2008), the leading policy document for end-of-life in England and Wales, promotes improved healthcare service provision to enable all people to experience what is considered within the policy a 'good death'. The strategy notes that 'there are distressing reports of people not being treated with dignity and respect' and that people may not be able to die in their place of choice (p. 9). Therefore, the creation of English EOLC policy has been interpreted as a response to publicised negative experiences of dying people (Seymour, 2012). These reports provide a contemporary example of the critiques levelled at dying in institutions several decades ago (e.g. Illich, 1976), indicating that despite advances in medical technologies, care for the dying more generally has not necessarily improved or indeed kept pace with demographic and epidemiological shifts, and that people continue to express dissatisfaction with how death is handled within biomedicine. In this article, I argue that EOLC policy-makers have interpreted such examples as forms of 'social death', where personhood is not respected, and have, in part, devised EOLC policy to reduce the possibly of this occurring. Coupled with a rise in consumerist healthcare more generally and the roots of EOLC in hospice philosophy, this has resulted in EOLC policy that promotes patient autonomy and agency to enable 'person-centred care'.

Although critiques have been made about current healthcare practices that may result in people not being treated with dignity, interpretable as a form of social death, this paper is concerned with how such practices are understood by policy-makers. Policy documents and discussions with policy-makers indicate what has come to be valued and how different kinds of experience and evidence are mobilised to promote changes in practice and thinking. Consequently, policy can be viewed as a social agent: the principles and guidelines embedded in documents and speeches are used to change the processes of healthcare practice and the ways in which experiences can be evaluated (e.g. Riles, 2006).

Barbour has suggested that medical professionals and policy-makers have borrowed from the social sciences through a process that she terms 'sociolization', which is most notable in the narrative turn within medicine (Barbour, 2011). Through this process, issues that have been raised within the social sciences – such as the importance of understanding a person's biography to understand their illness experience – have migrated from social theory into healthcare policy. This article analyses if, how and the extent to which theories around social death have found resonance within end-of-life care policy. In order to do this, I employ a discourse analysis of the English EOLC policy (understood loosely to include national guidelines, strategy documents and local articulates of national strategies). This included examining select policy documents (from 2008 to early 2015), fieldnotes from events that promoted implementation of the End of Life Care Strategy in 2010–2012, and 13 interviews with people involved in creating and informing EOLC policy in England; I refer to them as policy-makers, and quotes from them have been anonymised to protect confidentiality. Initial data collection and analysis were part of a larger study about choice in EOLC and a further description of methods can be found in Borgstrom (2014). Initial analysis, for this article, sought explicit references to the concept of social death and further analysis drew on the theoretical literature, which associates social death with a lack of personhood. I therefore identified occasions when policy-makers alluded to possible cases of social death, through descriptions of care that 'lacked dignity' or were 'distressing' or where personhood was somehow denied or not respected. Whilst these examples were not as frequently used within the policy discourse as the concept of 'good death' was (although they can be related), as I demonstrate below, they are used to mobilise and justify the need for particular elements of EOLC policy. In this way, part of the sociolization process is incorporating theoretical ideas about social death into the policy rhetoric.

In order to explore how policy-makers engage with the concept of social death in the context of EOLC, I first sketch what EOLC policy is and how it has been formed within England over the last couple of decades. I then discuss the data, providing examples of how social death was discussed by policy-makers and the conclusions they drew from their interpretations of occurrences or possibilities of social death (always prior to physiological death). The last section challenges the use of concept of social death by policy-makers – both how it is used and the ability of the proposed 'solutions' to counter the issues that concerned them.

End-of-life care policy

End-of-life care is a relatively new field of medicine that has its roots in cancer care, hospice philosophy and palliative medicine (Seymour, 2012), although it is applied more broadly across diagnoses and clinical settings beyond these specialities. Within England, approximately 500,000 die each year with most expected to have some EOLC or contact with health services towards the end of life (Hughes-Hallett, Craft, & Davies, 2011). To address the care of the dying, end-of-life care is promoted through national policy, specifically the End of Life Care Strategy (Department of Health, 2008). This sought to change the provision of care for dying persons, improving access and quality across the country regardless of diagnosis or healthcare setting. In interviews, a wide range of policy-makers said that the purpose of the strategy was to 'affect change' and to 'take the excellent and make it the norm'. The strategy focused on patient choice and home death, and acted as a lever for changes in practice and related government policies, such as how to fund health and social care (Borgstrom, 2016).

Growing out of the National Health Service (NHS) Next Stage Review (House of Commons Health Committee, 2008), disease-specific frameworks (e.g. Department of Health, 2001), and work done by the relatively new National End of Life Care Programme, the strategy was developed within the Department of Health. Members of the advisory board and working groups who developed the policy were primarily not civil servants but came from diverse professional backgrounds, including the third sector, academic research and those with professional and/or personal experience in palliative and end-of-life care. Developing policy was viewed by those interviewed as a collaborative process, with many opportunities for 'partnerships', which nevertheless involved negotiating values and priorities. Policy-makers described their role as promoting 'best practice' to address patient and professional experience of daily practice and 'what they know needs improving', and thought about how they could 'add value' to what already happens. For example, Jenny (a clinician and researcher who was involved since the initial discussions about national policy in this field) described creating EOLC policy (and consequent service re-development) as 'a way of changing things so the right things happen at the right time'. The resulting outcome from the strategy was a three-prong approach to the care of the dying: a care pathway with an emphasis on early identification and communication about dying and managed care, raising national awareness about dying and improving professional education and funding.

Four annual reviews have been published marking the progress made from implementing the End of Life Care Strategy (Department of Health, 2009, 2010, 2011, 2012). Year-on-year there have been improvements across all indicators of quality in EOLC as defined by policy-makers (M. Richards, 2014), yet several high-profile reports, including the removal of the Liverpool Care Pathway previously promoted by EOLC policy, suggest that care of the dying has not consistently improved across the country, and that many people do not experience a 'good death' as end-of-life care policy guidelines suggest (Dixon, King, Matosevic, Clark, & Knapp, 2015; Neuberger et al., 2013; Parliamentary and Health Service Ombudsman, 2015). End of life care policy is being continuously revised, but related consultations suggest that patient choice and dignity will remain important themes (The Choice in End of Life Care Programme Board, 2015).

Social death within end-of-life care policy

As policy-makers are continuously engaging with wider social changes and debates, and some of them are academic and clinical researchers, it can be expected that their draws on ideas informed by social issues and theory. The evidence for this flow of ideas can be found in both explicit references to theoretical concepts or more implicitly in how issues are framed and discussed. In this section, I outline how 'social death' is mobilised by policy-makers as a possible occurrence in daily clinical practice in order for them to make arguments about changing how dying persons are cared for.

The term 'social death' does not feature within the national End of Life Care Strategy, and perhaps it would be unreasonable to expect it to be in the policy document text. Firstly, within academia there is a considerable debate and variation about what the term means and who it applies to (Sweeting & Gilhooly, 1992); such ambiguity may not be useful when setting out guidelines for healthcare. Secondly, policy documents have their own kind of language (Corson, 1988) and EOLC policy is targeted at an interdisciplinary audience; therefore it is understandable that policy-makers have not adopted what can be viewed as social science 'jargon' in a healthcare document. However, if the concept has informed the thinking of policy-makers, either direct or indirect references to it (or even references to academic literature discussing the idea) can indicate its influence in thinking about the care of the dying. This is particularly pertinent in texts and events around main policy initiatives that seek to educate practitioners about the intention and direction of policy.

For example, within a book that outlines how the End of Life Care Strategy can be operationalised, the authors, who are all part of the National Council of Palliative Care (an organisation that informs and promotes EOLC policy), sets out the policy and strategy within the 'context and philosophy of end of life care' (Hayes et al., 2014). One chapter explains the need for EOLC policy in England and the rationale behind it, drawing considerably on sociological references, including medicalisation critiques and the changing nature of dying in society. As part of this, there is over a page dedicated to describing 'social death and marginalised dying' (pp. 15–16). The authors note the historical origins of the term in Sudnow's (1967) work and suggest that social death is 'a phenomenon that can be as real today as it was when first observed' (p. 15). So whilst the term social death does not feature directly in the End of Life Care Strategy, its inclusion in this book suggests that it has informed the construction of contemporary EOLC policy, or at least is being used to justify a need to change practices.

In my analysis, there were three ways in which social death was discussed by policy-makers in the context of EOLC policy; each approach has its own section below. Each way of discussing social death was mobilised by policy-makers to do something different by highlighting specific aspects about death, dying and care that needed (from their perspective) addressing. In doing so, each version or possibility of social death asserts different values and serves to illustrate the connections policy-makers were making and creating between thinking about death, personhood and care practices.

Exclusion, isolation and advance care planning

The first category includes a direct reference to social death and sociological literature on the topic, including how the concept of social death has been merged with notions about marginalisation and isolation, drawing on the book mentioned above. In the book section, social death is identified in people being 'gradually removed from mainstream society … [and] may accompany isolation and loss of a sense of being' (Hayes et al., 2014, p. 15). Specific research from the late 1990s and early 2000s on older people and care homes is cited to describe how care of the dying may result in the exclusion of the dying person. Social death is identified as a result of a series of processes that separate the person from the body whilst also marginalising the person's agency and ability to interact in society. In effect, these examples highlighted how people were, as a result of the care they received, no longer being viewed as active agents in their own lives. Since EOLC is based on a holistic, person-centred philosophy that seeks to treat and care for the 'whole person', this kind of social death occurring before physical death is problematic as it signifies that person-centred care is not being delivered or realised. Such reduction in interaction before bodily death is interpreted within this context as being premature, and therefore socially and morally inappropriate.

The book's authors note that the hospice movement, which has strongly influenced end-of-life care policy, has 'sought to counter this exclusion of people who are dying' through an emphasis on living until death (Hayes et al., 2014, p. 16). End-of-life care then is implied as an appropriate response, or even preventive measure, to social death. Readers of the book are encouraged to think about people they know currently receiving care who may be the subject of 'social death' and how they can 'turn exclusion into inclusion' (p. 16). As the purpose of the book is to suggest how to apply the EOLC strategy to provide person-centred care, further reading of the text suggests that in this context potential solutions include openly talking about death, especially to facilitate advance care planning.

Advance care planning encourages people to make statements about treatment decisions in advance of those decisions being required (Thomas & Lobo, 2011). In the context of EOLC, it is used as a way of opening up conversations between staff, patients and families about what the dying process may entail, and how it can be managed (Waldrop & Meeker, 2012). People are encouraged to write declarations of their 'choices' for care and treatment by actively imagining what dying and death may be like. For example, within the Preferred Priorities for Care document that is endorsed by national EOLC policy, people are asked 'what are your preferences and priorities for your future care' (Storey & Betteley, 2011). In the interviews I conducted, policy-makers suggested that people could think of elements of care from 'the room you're in', 'what's on the telly', to refusing certain treatments. Making such choices – and having them respected by others – was stated by policy-makers as evidence of 'living until death' and therefore an element of personhood.

Importantly, healthcare professionals are encouraged to consult these documents and patients' wishes when making treatment decisions (Wilson et al., 2013), rejecting a more paternalistic model of care. By emphasising the importance of advance care planning as part of the larger end-of-life care pathway, the role of patient autonomy throughout the journey is stressed within the policy discourse. The patient is viewed as having an active voice and decision-making capabilities to affect the kind of care they receive (Thomas & Lobo, 2011). Sarah, who worked within a national disease-related charity, stated that care should reflect patient choice 'as they are still a person ... [even if] capacity diminishes, emotions don't diminish'. This in turn changes dying from something that is strictly clinically managed and done to the body, to something that engages and is in line with the patient's sensibilities. As summed up by Jenny, a marker of good care at the end of life is care that it is 'aligned with people's preferences', which she, like other policy-makers, assumed and advocated can be done through advance care planning. The connection between choice and quality of care is further stated in more recent policy documents, like in the review of choice in end of life care, which unequivocally stated that there is a link between 'high quality end of life care' and people's care choices (The Choice in End of Life Care Review Board, 2015, p. 13). Through this logic, respecting patient choice is equated to respecting the person, which in turn is a signifier and lever of good care and means a premature social death is less likely to occur.

Inequality, equity and social death

The second category is from the same source, although it also came up in the interviews, and includes a direct reference to social death and social science literature on the topic. Within the policy discourse, social death was not something that all patients are at risk of experiencing. There is a particular concern that certain sub-groups of the population, such as older persons who experience frailty or those dying from non-malignant conditions, may be at greater risk of poor end-of-life care that ignores their dying or treats them as if dead (Hayes et al., 2014). To support these claims, sociological and anthropological studies of care and dying are cited (e.g. Froggatt, 2001; Hockey, 1990; Komaromy, 2000).

For example, Froggatt (2001) and Hockey's (1990) work in care homes is referenced to highlight how care home staff manage dying as decline by placing people in other rooms. The authors of the book note that language used to refer to people can serve to mark this transition and social death. Similarly, they suggest such practices can occur as 'communication and interaction with the person who is dying become increasingly difficult' (Hayes et al., 2014, p. 15). Whilst these examples may apply primarily to older persons (without mentioning potential ageism) who experience frailty and dementia, it is implied within the text that people who have other conditions – such as neurological conditions – may also have similar 'isolating' experiences.

This is a concern for policy-makers as patients who have non-malignant conditions have, historically, not had as much support from palliative care services compared to those dying of cancer, and are less likely to have done advance care planning (Ahmed, Bestall, Ahmedzai, Payne, & Noble, 2004; Walshe, Todd, Caress, & Chew-Graham, 2009). This is a particular concern, as Sarah noted in an interview, for patients who may 'lose capacity as cognitive function declines'. These concerns are supported by recent research highlighting the varying levels of access across diseases (Dixon et al., 2015). Although not fully articulated in the texts or interviews, what is at stake in this reference to social death is that healthcare professionals treat dying people differently based on their diagnosis, even if people have similar clinical and supportive needs. Since policy-makers are seeking to promote the use of EOLC for all, highlighting sub-groups who may not have access, and noting that this access may be a result of care practices that negate their personhood, serves to demonstrate a need to re-design and re-align healthcare practices.

Good death, dignity, and communication

The last category encompasses inferences about social death in relation to concepts such as 'good death' and 'dignity'; whilst these are highly problematic in themselves, they are treated as readily understood and shared values within the policy discourse (Borgstrom, 2014, 2016). In the policy events and interviews with policy-makers, it was not unusual for people to refer to examples where the quality of care was not optimal as part of their discussions about why EOLC policy was needed. These were often quickly contrasted to what a 'good death' could be, which is first and foremost defined as being treated as 'an individual, with dignity and respect' (Department of Health, 2008, p. 9) in the End of Life Care Strategy. The way in which people drew on these examples highlighted ways in which dying people and their families may not be treated as persons within the healthcare system, or where professionals have 'turned away' from death and dying, perhaps viewing it as a failure (Richards, 2008).

For example, one interviewee, John (a doctor and national policy representative) referred to a tabloid newspaper article about an older woman being treated as a 'slab of meat' by healthcare professionals in a hospital, leading to her not having a 'good death' as reported and interpreted by John. The article implied that, from the family's perspective at least, the hospital staff did not adequately care for the woman, treating her as an object, and considered their mother as already dead. Whilst I have heard such scenarios re-interpreted by healthcare professionals as conforming to guidance (particularly prior to the Liverpool Care Pathway being withdrawn), John stated that no one should have such an experience or feel like that is what has happened. In this context, (a premature) social death can be understood as not being adequately cared for and therefore preventing a good death, however defined, at the end of life.

Instead, he suggested that staff need to communicate their actions and intentions with patients and families better, 'explaining the process of death to them'. He did not deny that such scenarios can occur, or that it may be a form of neglect; he suggested that it was a result of miscommunication and misunderstanding between families and professionals, which serves to give the impression that healthcare professionals do not treat dying patients as persons. As an alternative, John suggested that there is a need to change public expectations and professional caring practices to be more open about dying. His logic was that such openness would counter the interpretation of care highlighted in the tabloid headline. Therefore, it is not the care practices themselves that are at stake here or the cause of social death; instead, they have been reduced to (mis)communication.

This mode of 'open awareness' as several policy-makers referred to it (explicitly drawing on Glaser and Strauss' theory of awareness contexts – see Glaser & Strauss, 1965) requires healthcare professionals to identify dying earlier and to openly communicate with patients and families that death is likely and approaching (Leadership Alliance for the Care of Dying People, 2014; National Council for Palliative Care & Dying Matters, 2011). For instance, the General Medical Council's advice is that doctors discuss end-of-life care with patients well in advance of the person's last few days (GMC, 2010). Sociological research about the effectiveness of open awareness and documenting patient preferences about the end of life is used within policy documents and events to provide evidence for the ability of this kind of care practice to enable patients to be persons up until their bodily death (e.g. Seale, Addington-Hall, & McCarthy, 1997). Essentially, policy-makers believe that 'people want to deliver good care' (Jenny) and 'empowering people to talk … is fundamental to good end of life care' (Hayes et al., 2014, p. 37).

In order to promote better communication at the end of life, John, like other policy-makers, suggested that training in EOLC needs to improve across all healthcare professions. Amy, who led policy for a national palliative care-oriented charity and actively lobbied government, said that her organisation pushed for 'mandatory training in end-of-life care' when discussing national policy with politicians and civil servants. Not only would training help address patient dignity issues, she considered it vital to addressing staff burnout and organisationally readdressing priorities that may lead to uncaring practices. Steve, who had a role similar to that of Amy, suggested that many healthcare professionals had a 'lack of confidence' that may mean they do not talk or engage with patients, inadvertently causing them to provide sub-standard care. Policy-makers such as Steve and Amy use case examples of 'bad care' and studies that demonstrate undertraining and professional taboos around death to persuade politicians that care of the dying needs reforming. Encouraging discussions about death, dying and bereavement was viewed as a way to improve the professional and political awareness of these topics. A focus on EOLC education and openly discussing dying, not just within clinical practice but more generally as well, is consequently viewed by some policy-makers as a direct way to alter organisational and societal processes that may lead to 'social death'.

Overall

The above examples of how policy-makers discuss social death demonstrate how policy-makers can think of social death as an occurrence and a potential regular practice, both of which are viewed as antithetical to 'good' end-of-life care. Framing social death as problematic then provides an avenue for opening up a public and professional discussion about what care of the dying looks like and should look like. Bringing the idea of social death explicitly or implicitly to the fore enables policy-makers to make claims about what needs to change in current end-of-life care to enable people to be treated as persons until they die and to enable them to have a 'good death'. The solutions suggested by policy-makers, unsurprisingly, support the philosophical roots of end-of-life care policy that view best care as holistic, patient-centred and supportive of patient autonomy. By referring to instances where social death may occur, policy-makers are effectively highlighting gaps in current or past practice that does not align with the philosophy and practice of care they are advocating. Policy-makers suggest then that EOLC policy, promoting increased training and communication, can readdress issues of social death by asserting the centrality of the person – through communication – during the transition from actively living to being dead. As Jenny said, she hoped EOLC policy promoting advance care planning would 'prevent medicalisation of dying … [by enabling people to] live in the context of their dying'. Ultimately, social death is mobilised by policy-makers within end-of-life care discussions to provide an impetus for changing care practices in a way that frames dying as a trajectory that can result in a good death.

Discussion

It is commendable that policy-makers actively want to improve the experience of people who are dying, and have acknowledged that previous critiques resulted from how care was managed. By looking at how policy-makers engage with the concept of social death and how they mobilise it to justify aspects of end-of-life care policy, it is apparent that it is being used to portray particular understandings of what it means to be a person and what sociality is like. Policies that seek to minimise the likelihood of a person experiencing social death before physical death focus on the patient's agency and communication. However, these ideas of social death do not address the core of Sudnow's original critique when he coined the term 'social death', which argued that social death results from a focus on the body. This section outlines this disconnect and suggests that it provides an explanation for continued critiques of the care of the dying.

The alternatives or solutions to prevent social death, as suggested by policy-makers, focus around advance care planning, equal access to care, and communication and training about dying. At the heart of these, and within the national End of Life Care Strategy more generally, lies the thread that talking about dying can improve the care and experience of death. In the context of social death, such talk can serve to re-align social death and physiological death, so the logic goes, by enabling, for example, preferences to be expressed and followed, and for professionals to educate patients and families about the dying process. In this sequence, communication is tied with agency – being able to make information known and to enable others to act accordingly – and policy-makers connect these intrinsically with 'dignified care'. If social death is understood theoretically as representing a loss of personhood, in these examples, agency (or being treated as if one has little agency within the healthcare system) and the ability to verbally exchange information are viewed within this context as key elements of personhood that are at risk of being prematurely 'lost' towards the end of life.

At this point, this way of describing and responding to social death is consistent with the social science literature of the late 1990s and early 2000s, which policy-makers draw on. However, policy-makers also make reference to Sudnow's work and it is here that I wish to problematize the use of social death in this context and the over-emphasis on communication and preference as expression of sociality and personhood. Sudnow's original work on social death was about how practices may change as a result of healthcare professionals recognising and prognosticating dying and death, which is a core element of end-of-life care. Spotting that there was a phasing out of the attention given to dying patients, Sudnow (1967) defined social death as the point 'at which a patient is treated essentially as a corpse' (p. 74) although his/her body may still be physiologically functioning. This definition of social death serves to outline the practices, within the hospital settings under study, that mark how socially relative attributes of the person ceased to be operative in the way staff interacted with patients. For example, he describes how autopsy permits were filed and obtained from relatives before a person died, pre-empting a patient's death. It is apparent in Sudnow's writing that social death is not just about an asocial treatment of the person per se, but the increasing importance of *the body* as the focal object in how the patient is discussed and how the dying process is managed. Others have proposed that biomedicine marginalises both the people and the processes involved in dying and caring for the dying as it does not know how to handle death in the absence of a cure or does not have the ability to restore the body's functioning (Christakis, 2001).

The examples of social death provided by policy-makers highlight the asocial treatment of the dying person; however, as the examples stand and are interpreted by policy-makers, they do not go as far as to suggest that social death can be the result of medicalised dying, where the body is foregrounded in care practices. Another interpretation of the 'slab of meat' case could read that staff were focusing on biomedical care, which to the family at least appeared as dehumanised treatment. I am not trying to justify their actions or privilege one interpretation over another; instead, I make this observation to highlight the selective ways in which policy-makers engage with the concept of social death. In doing so, they are able to suggest solutions that consider a particular version of what 'being social' means – expressing preferences and engaging in communication – rather than problematize how the care of the dying can and does see the dying body as an object.

End-of-life care is often cited as being person-centred (Hayes et al., 2014), and in the practice of caring for the dying, healthcare professionals are tasked with managing decline and the elements of personhood discussed above, including agency. End-of-life policy is said to have come of age in England with the release of the national strategy in 2008, and there has been some evidence that advance care planning and the EOLC strategy have enabled more people to have 'good deaths' (Department of Health, 2012). Yet there have been several high-profile scandals about poor care of the dying since then. This includes the Mid-Staffordshire scandal where poor care was leading to higher than average mortality rates within the hospital and the retraction of the Liverpool Care Pathway. This is perhaps suggestive that the kind of care management that can lead to premature social death, as feared by EOLC policy-makers, has continued, despite changes in EOLC policy and training. This is partly due to a wider healthcare culture that focuses on procedure rather than on processes or persons (Napier et al., 2014; Neuberger et al., 2013; The Mid Staffordshire NHS Foundation Trust Public Inquiry, 2013); perhaps a longer period since the release of the End of Life Care Strategy is needed to evaluate its ability to change practices. Nevertheless, although there has been some progress in changing the care of the dying to promote person-centred care, there are still instances that could be described as (premature) social death within the NHS today.

Healthcare practice can still result in instances of social death because EOLC policy and practice is built around a notion that bodily death is an identifiable and definable event, around which care can be organised (Froggatt, 2007, p. 243). This lies at the core of Sudnow's critique of how dying persons were cared for. The actions promoted by EOLC policy as a way of negating social death involve people to be aware of their terminal condition, to plan for their future care, and to openly talk about their preferences. However, it is the assessment of the patient's body by professionals that drives this care management, noting aspects that are important to the medical and palliative care model rather than what might be important to the dying person (Kellehear, 2009). Even where patient preference is trumpeted, through processes such as advance care planning and the ability to provide care towards the end of life that is in line with patient choice, the emphasis in (primarily) on how to manage the dying body. This stance is part of an institutional agenda that enables efficient management of dying people and their preferences (Green, 2008). Medical systems have a 'vested interest in people being aware of their impending deaths' (Pery & Wein, 2008, p. 400). Yet, this approach does not adequately accommodate those who may wish to not participate in advance care planning (Barclay, Momen, Case-Upton, Kuhn, &

Smith, 2011) nor does it realise the messiness of the dying experience (Strange, 2009). Fundamentally, although EOLC seeks to draw on patient preferences, there is a still a strong focus on the management of the dying body, evident in the EOLC strategy and suggestion that there needs to be better communication and training about what dying is like.

I would argue, however, that focusing on communication and advance care planning, in and of themselves, will not manage to change how healthcare professionals (or care home staff, etc.) orient themselves to the care of the dying. These policies go some way in promoting a different way of thinking and approaching the care of the dying, that seeks to foreground the dying person, but do not address the nature of dying and the clinical care practices that seek to manage physiological changes. For this to occur, policy-makers need to challenge themselves using Sudnow's original critique and the medical treatment of persons as bodies, rather than focus on an understanding of social death that rests primarily with personhood and agency.

Conclusion

The concept of social death is used to describe an ontological deficit of the person. Policy-makers working in EOLC have drawn on the concept of social death in devising and justifying policy recommendations to change the care of the dying. In their interpretations, social death can occur from care practices that exclude the dying person and may disproportionally affect people dying from non-malignant conditions. To address this, EOLC policy suggests involving patients in planning for their care and place of death and increasing awareness about death and dying. Agency, supported by information, is therefore considered to be key elements of personhood. However, these interpretations of social death and personhood uphold mind/body dualism (despite being part of 'person-centred care') and the solutions do not in and of themselves radically challenge the foregrounding of the body in the care of the dying.

Acknowledgements

I am grateful for the organisers of the Centre for Death and Society (CDAS) conference focusing on social death and the helpful comments I received from the audience as well as the reviewers and editors of this special issue. Simon Cohn's astute questions during my doctoral work helped me problematize the idea of social death.

Funding

The PhD research was funded by the National Institute of Health Research (NIHR), Collaboration for Leadership in Applied Heath Research and Care (CLAHRC) for Cambridgeshire and Peterborough. Time to write this paper was supported by the Foundation for the Sociology of Health and Illness Mildred Blaxter Post-Doctoral fellowship.

SOCIAL DEATH

References

Ahmed, N., Bestall, J. C., Ahmedzai, S. H., Payne, S. A., & Noble, B. (2004). Systematic review of the problems and issues of accessing specialist palliative care by patients, carers and health and social care professionals. *Palliative Medicine, 18*(6), 525–542.

Barbour, R. S. (2011). The biographical turn and the "sociolization" of medicine. *Medical Sociology Online, 6*(1), 15–25.

Barclay, S., Momen, N., Case-Upton, S., Kuhn, I., & Smith, E. (2011). End-of-life care conversations with heart failure patients: A systematic literature review and narrative synthesis. *British Journal of General Practice, 61*(582), 49–62.

Borgstrom, E. (2014). *Planning for death? An ethnographic study of English end-of-life care.* Cambridge: University of Cambridge. Retrieved from https://www.repository.cam.ac.uk/handle/1810/245560

Borgstrom, E. (2016). End of life care strategy and the coalition government. In L. Foster & K. Woodthrope (Eds.), *Death and social policy in challenging times.* Basingstoke: Palgrave Macmillan.

The Choice in End of Life Care Programme Board. (2015). *What's important to me: A review of choice in end of life care.* London: Author.

Christakis, N. A. (2001). *Death foretold: Prophecy and prognosis in medical care.* Chicago, IL: University of Chicago Press.

Clark, D. (2002). Between hope and acceptance: The medicalisation of dying. *British Medical Journal, 324,* 905–907.

Corson, D. (1988). Making the language of education policies more user-friendly. *Journal of Education Policy, 3*(3), 249–260.

Department of Health. (2001). *The NHS cancer plan.* London: Crown.

Department of Health. (2008). *End of life care strategy.* London: Crown.

Department of Health. (2009). *End of life care strategy: First annual report.* London: Crown.

Department of Health. (2010). *End of life care strategy: Second annual report.* London: Crown.

Department of Health. (2011). *End of life care strategy: Third annual report.* London: Crown.

Department of Health. (2012). *End of life care strategy: Fourth annual report.* London: Crown.

Dixon, J., King, D., Matosevic, T., Clark, M., & Knapp, M. (2015). *Equity in the provision of palliative care in the UK: Review of evidence.* London: LSE.

Froggatt, K. (2001). Life and death in English nursing homes: Sequestration or transition? *Ageing and Society, 21*(3), 319–332.

Froggatt, K. (2007). The "regulated death": A documentary analysis of the regulation and inspection of dying and death in English care homes for older people. *Ageing and Society, 27*(2), 233–247.

General Medical Council. (2010). *Treatment and care towards the end of life: Good practice in decision making.* London: Author.

Glaser, B. G., & Strauss, A. L. (1965). *Awareness of dying.* Chicago, IL: Aldine.

Green, J. W. (2008). *Beyond the good death: The anthropology of modern dying.* Philadelphia: University of Pennsylvania Press.

Hayes, A., Henry, C., Holloway, M., Lindsey, K., Sherwen, E., & Smith, T. (2014). *Pathways through care at the end of life.* London: Jessica Kingsley.

Hockey, J. (1990). *Experiences of death: An anthropological account.* Edinburgh: Edinburgh University Press.

House of Commons Health Committee. (2008). *NHS next stage review.* London: Crown.

Hughes-Hallett, T., Craft, A., & Davies, C. (2011). *Palliative care funding review: Funding the right care and support for everyone.* London: Department of Health.

Illich, I. (1976). *Limits to medicine; medical nemsis: The expropriation of health.* Harmondsworth: Penguin.

Kellehear, A. (2009). *The study of dying.* Cambridge: Cambridge University Press.

Komaromy, C. (2000). The sight and sound of death: The management of dead bodies in residential and nursing homes. *Mortality, 5*(3), 299–315.

Lawton, J. (2000). *The dying process: Patients' experiences of palliative care.* London: Routledge.

Leadership Alliance for the Care of Dying People. (2014). *One chance to get it right: Improving people's experience of care in the last few days and hours of life* London: Department of Health.

The Mid Staffordshire NHS Foundation Trust Public Inquiry. (2013). *Retrieved from the mid Staffordshire NHS Foundation Trust Public Inquiry.* London: Department of Health.

Murray, S. A., Kendall, M., Boyd, K., & Sheikh, A. (2005). Illness trajectories and palliative care. *British Medical Journal, 330,* 1007–1011.

Napier, A. D., Ancarno, C., Butler, B., Calabrese, J., Chater, A., Chatterjee, H., … Woolf, K. (2014). Culture and health. *The Lancet, 384*(9954), 1607–1639.

National Council for Palliative Care, & Dying Matters. (2011). *Dying – Doing it better*. London: Author.

Neuberger, J., Aaronovitch, D., Bonser, T., Charlesworth-Smith, D., Cox, D., Guthrie, C., … Waller, S. (2013). *More care, less pathway: A review of the liverpool care pathway*. London: Independent Review of the Liverpool Care Pathway; Crown.

Parliamentary and Health Service Ombudsman. (2015). *Dying without dignity*. London: Author.

Pery, S., & Wein, S. (2008). The dying patient: The right to know versus the duty to be aware. *Palliative & Supportive Care, 6*(4), 397–401.

Richards, M. (2008). *The End of Life Care Strategy: Promoting high quality care for all adults at the end of life*. London: Department of Health.

Richards, M. (2014a). Foreword. In A. Hayes, C. Henry, M. Holloway, K. Lindsey, E. Sherwen, & T. Smith (Eds.), *Pathways through care at the end of life* (pp. 9–10). London: Jessica Kingsley.

Richards, N. (2014b). The death of right-to-die campaigners. *Anthropology Today, 30*(3), 14–17.

Riles, A. (2006). *Documents: Artifacts of modern knowledge*. Ann Arbor, MI: The University of Michigan Press.

Seale, C., Addington-Hall, J., & McCarthy, M. (1997). Awareness of dying: Prevalence, causes and consequences. *Social Science & Medicine, 45*(3), 477–484.

Seymour, J. (2012). Looking back, looking forward: The evolution of palliative and end-of-life care in England. *Mortality, 17*(1), 1–17.

Spiro, M. (1996). Facing death. In H. M. Spiro, M. G. McCrea Curnen, & L. P. Wandel (Eds.), *Facing death: Where culture, religion, and medicine meet* (pp. xv–xx). New Haven: Yale University Press.

Storey, L., & Betteley, A. (2011). Preferred priorities for care: An advance care planning process. In K. Thomas & B. Lobo (Eds.), *Advance care planning in end of life care* (pp. 125–131). Oxford: Oxford University Press.

Strange, J.-M. (2009). Historical approaches to dying. In A. Kellehear (Ed.), *The study of dying* (pp. 123–146). Cambridge: Cambridge University Press.

Sudnow, D. (1967). *Passing on: The social organization of dying*. Upper Saddle River, NJ: Prentice-Hall.

Sweeting, H. N., & Gilhooly, M. L. M. (1992). Doctor, am I dead? A review of social death in modern societies. *Omega: Journal of Death and Dying, 24*(4), 251–269.

Thomas, K., & Lobo, B. (2011). *Advance care planning in end of life care*. Oxford: Oxford University Press.

Waldrop, D. P., & Meeker, M. A. (2012). Communication and advanced care planning in palliative and end-of-life care. *Nursing Outlook, 60*(6), 365–369.

Walshe, C., Todd, C., Caress, A., & Chew-Graham, C. (2009). Patterns of access to community palliative care services: A literature review. *Journal of Pain and Symptom Management, 37*(5), 884–912.

Wilson, C. J., Newman, J., Tapper, S., Lai, S., Cheng, P. H., Wu, F. M., & Tai-Seale, M. (2013). Multiple locations of advance care planning documentation in an electronic health record: Are they easy to find? *Journal of Palliative Medicine, 16*(9), 1089–1094. doi:10.1089/jpm.2012.0472

Post-mortem social death – exploring the absence of the deceased

Annika Jonsson

Department of Social and Psychological Studies, Karlstad University, Karlstad, Sweden

> The concept of social death is commonly used to describe how individuals or groups are condemned to existential homelessness at the outskirts of ordinary, human society. This article, however, explores social death as post-mortem phenomenon in contemporary Sweden. It is well known that lives may be extended beyond the grave through the practices and beliefs of the living, but not all the dead gain a social existence. For various reasons the living may not wish or be able to construe continuing bonds with their deceased, and as a consequence the deceased disappear from social life. Depending on the circumstances, this could be painful to or a relief for the living. It may also go unnoticed. Based on both individual and group interviews, this article investigates why some face post-mortem social death and others do not, and what shades of post-mortem social death there might be.

Introduction

In this article the concept of continuing bonds, commonly used to analyse relationships between the living and the dead, is also applied to trace the lack of such relationships. Continuing bonds grant the deceased a social life, since these bonds make them matter here and now in various respects. Lack of such bonds, in contrast, results in post-mortem social death for the deceased. As we shall see, it is not always a question of either or – there is a liminal space in between, where the deceased are in a social sense both alive and dead. The analysis is based on an interview study conducted in Sweden 2013–2015 with 28 participants in all. The key concepts of the article will be discussed below.

The social death concept has been used in different contexts to denote how people are unable to sustain identity and a sense of meaning, due to social, sometimes physical, isolation and to loss of control over their own life and (Bauman, 1992; Glaser & Strauss, 1966; Sudnow, 1967). Goffman (1959, p. 152) describes how categories of 'non-persons' are 'treated in their presence as if they were not there', for instance, the very young and the very old. Patterson (1982) makes a valuable contribution when clarifying how slaves, although condemned to social death, are still part of society in certain regards. They are marginalised but at the same time integrated, and Patterson (1982, p. 48) refers to this as 'the slave's liminal status'. Most of the research on social death concentrates solely on the living, and for good reasons, but this article explores social death as a post-mortem phenomenon.

Guenther (2013, p. xx, italics in original), analysing solitary confinement, says that the lives of individuals suffering social death 'no longer bear a social meaning; they no longer counts as lives that *matter*'. Lacking Patterson's liminality, this notion nevertheless bridges the gap between the living and the dead since a person's life, after as well as before physical death, may cease to matter. Guenther also suggests that social death occurs when a person is cut off from kin (all significant others, presumably) and prohibited from creating meaningful relationships that allows their existence to transcend the present. Social death is thus about being '*isolated in one's individuality*' (Guenther, 2013, p. xxiii, italics in original), that is, about being reduced to biological existence.

Guenther's argument reveals the two-sidedness of the concept – on the one hand it is about how people are perceived and treated, on the other hand it is about the experiences of those perceived and treated in certain ways. Unifying the different usages of the concept is, however, the recognition of an overarching asymmetrical relationship. In the context of slavery, Patterson (1982, p. 335) terms this 'a relation of parasitism'. Social death pre-mortem is thus inflicted upon individuals and causes them harm. Even though it has been argued that the deceased, as ante-mortem persons, in fact can be harmed by the actions of the living (Pitcher, 1984; Scarre, 2012), this is not the focus of this article. What is of interest is instead how and why the deceased end up suffering social death, and what shades of social death there may be.

Post-mortem life through continuing bonds

The deceased are present in society by default, in institutions, art and much of the materiality we see every day. They are also the people we find in photo albums and get to know from stories told by those who remember. They are our significant others, intricately entangled in our lives and self-perceptions. In 1996, Klass et al. coined the term *continuing bonds* to draw positive attention to and legitimise the bonds that the living may maintain with their deceased. It was formulated as a critique of the main Western grief model which encourages people to let go of the deceased. The bonds can be private and/or public, that is, formed within the living due to, primarily, experiences of the deceased as somehow present or manifested in everyday conversations (Walter, 1996).

Continuing bonds constitute a multifaceted phenomenon. The living may actively intensify the presence of the deceased with the help of objects and photos (Gibson, 2008; Unruh, 1983), or by staying in a certain house or city (Francis, Kellaher, & Neophytou, 2005). They may also keep the person alive on Facebook (Church, 2013), or try to contact the person through spiritualist mediums (Walliss, 2001). When handling the loss, they sometimes turn to self-help groups where the deceased can be given a new form of existence within an understanding community (Klass, 1997). Bonds are also formed when the living strive to incorporate the ambitions of the deceased in their daily life, and recognise how they are shaped as persons by the deceased (Vickio, 1999). Apart from this, it is not very unusual, as Hallam, Hockey, and Howarth (1999) note, that the dead live a life of their own – scents and music can abruptly bring them back. Every now and then they even appear visually without any warnings. The living, albeit being the vehicle, are not necessarily in full control of these bonds then.

Researchers interested in continuing bonds have since 1996 (and before that, using other concepts) examined how the deceased are experienced as or made present. As a consequence, absence of the deceased remains largely unexplored. We might say that a silence surrounds social death post-mortem, or that the (apparent) disappearance of the deceased from the social is taken for granted in this part of the world.

Countries labelled as secularised, such as Sweden, seem to pose a particular challenge to researchers interested in continuing bonds and the role of the deceased. The lack of official rituals and tangible metaphysical framework creates something of a mystery. In Japan the deceased are transformed into ancestors through a series of rituals performed by the family (Klass & Goss, 1999) and among the Buryat, inhabiting the northeast Mongolian–Russian border, the deceased are believed to be reborn within a living kin. Each individual is thus comprised by a number of souls (Empson, 2007). Notions about what the dead are, what they can become and how they ought to be treated clearly differs; there is no evident way of dealing with these questions.

As Bennett and Bennett (2000, p. 154) show in their analysis of 'paranormal' experiences among bereaved in two English cities, people have access to two, competing discourses – the 'materialist' and the 'supernaturalist'. Depending on the situation, they either explain presence of and communication with the deceased as an illusion or as a fact. The authors conclude that formal surveys, embedded in the materialist discourse, are likely to result in materialist accounts. But the investigation reveals something else as well – the double nature of contemporary English culture when it comes to dealing with the dead. Day (2012), analysing data from a 10-year generational study also conducted in England, offers another possible interpretation. She is critical of the idea that afterlife beliefs need a religious foundation and suggests that we see them as ancestor veneration. Many of her interviewees, despite defining themselves as atheist or non-religious, happily talked about spirits and sensing the dead. According to Day (2012, p. 170) they are involved in 'extraordinary relationality'. She, however, does not offer a compelling explanation as to why some engage in this relationality and some do not. As a consequence, the absence (social death) of the ancestors/deceased remains untheorised.

The Swedish context

According to a survey carried out in Sweden in 2012 with 1000 respondents, one in five claimed to have been in contact with or sensed the presence of a deceased (Sifo, 2012). Another survey showed that in 2011, 51% of the respondents, 3096 in total, placed candles on graves on All Hallows Eve (Bromander, 2012). The questionnaire was, however, sent to 9000 so the number of people not responding was rather high. It is difficult to tell whether Swedish culture is changing and continuing bonds are being cultivated more freely, or if people are involved in quite traditional forms of ancestor veneration (cf. Day, 2012). While some assert that afterlife beliefs are more accepted today than in the 1970s (Sjödin, 2003), others suggest that the large quantitative studies constructed to map out such things are biased in problematic ways. Willander (2014) notes that most surveys attempt to categorise people in ways that does not capture their actual point of view, for instance, by assuming that church membership is significant.

Most Swedes are, af Burén (2015) asserts, semi-secular. Different religious and pop religious components are combined without effort or hesitation, at the same time as certain atheistic notions are embraced. af Burén proposes that semi-secular people do not feel the need to create coherent frameworks – they are casual, capricious (non)believers. Against this background it is extremely difficult to speculate about how continuing bonds and lack of continuing bonds may be related to 'spiritual', religious or atheist beliefs. And, as Day (2012) reminds us, relationality might be more important when we are to explain relationships between the living and the dead. According to the World Values Studies (2010), Sweden is the most individualised country in the world, meaning that the individual's autonomy is highly valued. Bauman (2007, p. 2) states that we find ourselves in a liquid phase of modernity where 'interhuman bonds (...) become increasingly frail and admitted to be temporary'. On the surface Sweden seems to be leading this race towards freedom and mobility, with 37.7% single households in 2012 (SCB, 2013), but, yet again, it is not easy to know what numbers and theories actually reveal. As Jamieson and Simpson (2013) point out, living alone is not necessarily related to a reduced social life or lack of closeness to others.

With no previous research to guide the way, it is not easily decided what else to take into account. There is of course research on grief and loss, but I have not been able to locate any studies conducted in Sweden on continuing bonds or absence of the dead. In an analysis of what shapes death practices, Walter (2012) touches upon, among other things, migration, inequality and technology. Such factors, and numerous others, most likely influence perceptions of and attitudes towards the dead, but empirical investigations must lead the way.

The interviews

The empirical material consists of 15 individual interviews and 4 group interviews conducted in Sweden with, all in all, 18 women and 10 men aged 25–80. Two thirds of the interviews were followed by mail conversations in which the interviewees clarified certain sentiments or word usages, or expanded their views on especially interesting topics. One of the interviews, conducted late in the process when the project was clearly outlined, was conducted solely by email. The first two group interviews were unexpectedly suggested by the interviewees. Because they proved fruitful, for instance, by providing me with *in situ* storytelling, the choice was made to conduct two more with alternative family constellations. I make no distinction between the individual and the group interviews in the analysis, mainly because careful attention was given to each individual in all of the interviews. The interviews are therefore, regardless of the number of participants, similar in style. The interaction that took place during the group interviews, however, exemplified what was being said, which adds to the material.

The interviewees differ in terms of family situation, experiences of death, religious/spiritual beliefs and occupational/educational background. Starting out, I asked a couple of acquaintances if they would consider talking to me and upon learning more about the project, they suggested others that could be of interest. It became a snowballing process with several balls. As Thompson (2002) points out, snowballing sampling can mean different things. It tends to be used when the population requested is hard to identify and researchers need the knowledge of the participants. In this case there was no particular population to identify, but I was looking for width in the interview material. As stated above, there is no research on continuing bonds/post-mortem social death in Sweden and therefore I wanted to capture as many angles as possible. Some of the variables listed above are not visible in the analysis presented, since their influence could not be determined. The interviews explored a number of themes, for instance, experiences of people dying, and how death had been dealt with within the family and among friends. The most important theme was experiences of the deceased as absent or/and present in interviewees' daily lives.

It has been debated whether accounts given in interviews are valid outside of the interview situation. Hammersley (2008), among others, discusses the tendency to treat interviewees as witnesses of what really happened. In cases where interviewees only communicate their own perceptions I suggest that, because of the multifacetedness of human experience, several, even contradictory, narratives can in fact be true at the same time. The analysis rests largely on the interviewees' emotional accounts. As Smart (2007) asserts, sociology often fails to take emotions seriously, even though they permeate many of the phenomena studied. When it comes to sensing absence and presence of the deceased, these experiences are usually conveyed in an emotional language. While the emotions are not named and categorised in the analysis, they are detectable in quotes from the interviews and the analytical approach per se.

During analysis, it also became evident that acts of storytelling needed to be acknowledged. Smart (2007, p. 83) says that storytelling 'builds a shared history and shared ancestry which makes the "new" generation belong (even if they feel uncomfortable or ultimately rebel)'. Storytelling, then, links people to each other as well as to events and places. The connectedness that storytelling results in is for many, she asserts, a presupposed part of life, while for adoptees, refugees and others it may not be. Creating connections between people, alive and dead, by telling stories is an active practice – if the storytelling ceases, the links between people start to dissolve.

SOCIAL DEATH

A parallel can be drawn to Carsten's (2007, p. 4) notion of 'everyday processes of relatedness', which underscores the importance of looking at that which seems almost too ordinary. As will be shown below, post-mortem life for the deceased to a large extent depends on storytelling as a continuing bond practice (Walter, 1996). Post-mortem social death, on the other hand, depends on the dissolving of connectedness, on stories never told.

Life post-mortem

To better understand what post-mortem social death entails, we will first look at how lives can be extended after (physical) death through continuing bonds. Some of the interviewees described such bonds, or relationships, as part of their everyday reality. Mother Elisabeth, 69, and daughter Ellen, 39, explained to me that uncle Carl would soon come cycling down the road and that Ellen's grandmother was probably in her garden, battling weeds with a cigarette in the corner of her mouth. Ellen and Elisabeth live next to each other on what they refer to as 'family ground', and although Carl has been dead for several months and grandmother Amanda died more than a decade ago, they remain present in conversations and imagination. 'They didn't turn into someone else just because they died,' as Elisabeth put it. Amanda, due to her contradictory nature and quirky habits, continues to be at the centre of some controversy as well as a steady source of inspiration to Ellen.

At the end of the interview, Elisabeth and Ellen reflected upon their habit of thinking and talking about the deceased as if they were still alive and humorously came to the conclusion that they might be a bit daft. 'It's like we don't quite get it,' Ellen remarked. To an outsider this might sound as if they are in denial about death, but they know fully well that Amanda and the others are dead. They just fail to see them as gone. Mitchell (2007, p. 1) emphasises the difference between the dead who are merely being remembered and the dead who 'play a lively part in our lives'. The continuing bonds that Ellen, Elisabeth and the rest of the family cultivate mean that the deceased still exercise a form of agency. They function as role model or antagonist, affecting the interaction between family members on a regular basis.

Sisters Jessica, 39, and Linda, 32, also belong to a family where the dead are given a social existence in various ways. Starting off, Linda asserted that 'we want the dead to live on, it's important to recognise that this is grandma's china'. When she later confessed that she in fact has few recollections of their grandma, Jessica stepped in and told an elaborate story about the pathos of their grandma. She then pointed out that Linda possesses the same pathos, thus strengthening the bond between Linda and her grandma.

Jessica, Linda, Ellen and Elisabeth all tell vivid stories that preserve the personalities and agendas of the now dead. In so doing they both access and contribute to what Kramer (2011, p. 392) terms the 'genealogical imaginary'. This imaginary is a collective, although sometimes contested, memory bank which allow people to, for example, tell stories about relatives that they have hardly met. Guenther (2013, p. xx) claims that 'social personhood' is constructed and maintained through a 'network of interconnected obligations, both in the present and extending into the past and future'. She argues that this is what is taken from persons suffering social death – the network that makes them a recognisable individual among other individuals. From a post-mortem perspective we could say that storytelling as a continuing bond practice situates the deceased in networks, thus granting them a social personhood.

Paula, 49, lost her husband, Leif, to Alzheimer's disease two years ago and described how, as the disease ran its course, she finally befriended his children and ex-wife. She used to feel threatened by the ex-wife and because the children always seemed to come first, they too became an obstacle. As Leif's health declined, they all made efforts to support each other and from this a new sense of connectedness emerged – they were transformed into an extended family. Paula stressed the importance of Leif's life-affirming personality in this, how they all were carried by it

SOCIAL DEATH

somehow. After his death she noticed how she changed on a personal level as well. She started prioritising her daughter and became more inclined to see what life had to offer, instead of what was missing. As Vickio (1999) points out, to adopt traits of the deceased and recognise this is a tangible way of keeping them alive.

A liminal existence

From a distance Alice, 25, appears to belong to the group outlined above. She talks about her deceased with other family members and trusted friends, she thinks about them a lot and is careful to keep photos and objects. Externally, not much separates her from Jessica and Linda. Up close, however, the image shifts. Unlike Jessica and the others, Alice does not partake in continuing bond practices that bring the deceased to life in a reassuring way. Life and death are held as absolute categories by Alice – people are either here or they are gone. While she acknowledges that the deceased live on in the actions and attitudes of the living, this is not given any weight. Her stories primarily convey irreconcilable loss and how every death shakes life to its foundations. At the time of the interview she reported not being 'actively grieving', the heavy emphasis on the absence of the deceased stems from a more general experience. She describes the anxiety she feels when she starts to forget the sound of people's voices and their unique gestures. There is indeed nothing strange about underlining absence – in a bodily sense the person is gone. What is strange, or interesting rather, is how the emphasis on absence results in a paradoxical presence of the deceased.

As Maddrell (2013, p. 506) notes, 'absence-presence is greater than the sum of the parts', that is, the experience of the dead as physically gone but emotionally present creates a particular mode with unique features. This mode is characterised by an 'experiential and relational tension' (Maddrell, 2013, p. 506) and this tension is noticeable in Alice's account. I suggest that the absence–presence constitutes a liminal existence for the deceased (cf. Patterson, 1982). They are not given a solid social existence in the same way as in the examples above, but neither have they disappeared. In moments they are very much present, but their possibilities for lasting presence is severely compromised by the emphasis on their physical absence. Turner (1969, p. 95) would call them 'threshold people', hinting at both the problems and the possibilities faced (by the living) within liminality. In one respect it is not only Alice's dead loved ones who have become threshold people, but Alice herself as well. She is 'betwixt and between' (Turner, 1969, p. 95) colliding experiences, emotions and aspirations. She says that she wants to remember everything about the deceased, but at the same time she is afraid of getting stuck in the past.

Liisa, 49, also embraces a life-death binary, perhaps more so than Alice. She sort of believes in an afterlife and that the deceased are not really lost, but is haunted by doubts. Trapped between the materialist and the supernaturalist discourses described by Bennett and Bennett (2000), she says 'I don't know if it's my inner dialogue or if it's the dead, I suspects it's my inner dialogue but I hope it's the dead talking to me.' She is familiar with Yalom's notion of rippling (2007), that is, that the dead continue to exist as ripples in lives lived here and now, but in her eyes that is not enough. Only an immortal soul will do, since 'humans have such a short memory'. Although she often talks to her dead, she is not always sure that they are there to listen. Overall this result in an absence–presence of the deceased that seems to leave Liisa uneasy albeit not as conflicted as Alice.

David, 40, provides us with yet another example. He gently places the deceased in the past, but accentuating their absence, what they no longer are, what they no longer can do, simultaneously echoes their presence. His description of his slightly rebellious grandmother, who used to invite him over for late nights of card playing and whisky, is very vivid and captures her absence–presence perfectly.

While there clearly are similarities between Alice, Liisa, David, and the others, the differences are quite distinct. What it seems to come down to is that Jessica, Linda, Elisabeth, Ellen and Paula

SOCIAL DEATH

are involved in continuing bond practices which mitigate the importance of the deceased's physical presence, alternatively an immortal soul of some sort. It is by no means a clear-cut picture, but it seems as if these practices build a new type of relationship. By using the concept of non-relationality, Henriksson (2014) draws attention to the way some relationships are practised in the shadow of the 'real' relationships. Henriksson (2014, p. 96, italics in original) asserts that 'practicing the *how* and *what* of not having a relationship to an ex-husband or ex-wife may mean that a person draws parallels to pre-divorce life'. Tentatively Alice and David, possibly Liisa as well, are practising a form of non-relationality which is modelled on the embodied interaction that they used to have with their now deceased. A consequence of this is that the deceased end up in liminality – they are neither what they used to be, nor have they transformed into something new.

A liminal existence turned into a social existence

Astrid, 70, lost her mother when she was 15. Her father soon remarried and the new wife did what she could to erase the traces of the former wife. Photos and clothes were stored away, and Astrid and her brother were encouraged not to speak of their mother. Astrid described herself as a young girl lost in an unintelligible world, bereaved but robbed of the possibility to work through her grief. That, she claimed, was the reason why she continued to mourn her mother until only a couple of years ago. Tired of sudden crying attacks and sorrow constantly giving life a darker shade, she then decided to face her mother. She visited places where the memories of her mother were strong and talked to relatives and other persons who knew her while she was alive. Although a difficult journey, it resulted in the realisation that her mother did not just die, she lived as well. She gave flowers to one of her husband's nieces and Astrid was taken to the garden were some of them still grew. This, among other things, proved that her mother in fact was not gone. Her traces were everywhere, even in Astrid herself as descriptions of her mother's personality allowed her to identify similarities between them.

As Cacho (2012) demonstrates, it can be difficult to grant some individuals a proper, social existence after death. When her cousin Brandon died in a car crash at age 19, he was labelled by society as just another deviant, drunk driving Latino. He did not have a promising job, a family of his own or a deeply agreeable personality. She writes (p. 149) 'Brandon was profoundly valued, but we could not tell you why.' Like Cacho, Astrid was for many years unable to find an appropriate place for her mother. She did not wrestle a racialised and in other ways normative narrative, but she did fight the idea that one should simply mourn and then move on. By piecing together her mother's life together with relatives and friends of the family, she appears to have developed a new relationality (Henriksson, 2014). The new relationality is based on the experience of her mother as, in numerous respects, present and is co-constructed with others. Walter (1996) stresses how a collective re/construction of the deceased's biography can grant the deceased a more stable position in the lives of the living. This certainly seems to be true in Astrid's case, as she is now able to say that she is missing her mother, but that her mother is no longer missing. The realisation that her mother was a wife, sister, friend, and so on, also provided Astrid with a deepened sense of her personhood. Valentine (2008) points out that it is not unusual for people to rediscover their deceased after a while, particularly when they come to understand how the person in various ways mattered to others.

Life in the margin

Some people more or less disappear when they die. Several of the interviewees recalled relatives, former friends and colleagues who vanished undramatically after physical death. Liisa, 49, made a clear distinction between persons who were gone-gone, 'they only exist in a stored away object or a quick thought', and persons who were just gone. The absence of those who were gone-gone was perfectly acceptable, expected even. Michael, 30, talked about a childhood friend who committed suicide five years ago and remarked that he hardly ever thinks about him anymore. Even though they had drifted apart somewhat by the time of his death, Michael seemed struck by his own indifference during the interview. Looking at these examples, it is obvious that people who are not embedded in the lives of others face post-mortem social death quite easily. When death practices in a society are less formal (Hallam & Hockey, 2001) and/or less religious (Klass & Walter, 2001), relationships with the dead may be chosen and depend, for instance, on how well people got on during life. How bruised the relationship was in life may also, as will be shown below, play a part.

Anders, 41, described his family as 'shattered, put through many ordeals, and tough'. When he grew up death was very much in the distance and those who died were rarely spoken of. To this day he 'doesn't feel the need to dwell on the deceased' and if they come to mind, there is almost always a particular, external reason. Most of the time, they are simply non-existent. His mother appears with some regularity, which he explains by the fact that she died quite recently and that they were family. Just like the others, however, she seldom appears without an external reminder and the visits tend to be brief. She suffered from alcoholism for many years and he says that it is nice not to have to worry about her anymore. Mulkay and Ernst (1991, p. 178) states that 'social death is the cessation of the individual person as an active agent in others' lives'. In line with this I propose that the deceased occupy a marginal space in Anders' life and basically have ceased to exert direct influence. They surface every now and then, but are not *experienced* as particularly significant for life here and now. They may of course still affect him in ways that he is not aware of. It seems clear that no continuing bond practices have been passed down from the older generation to him in the form of, for instance, a storytelling tradition. It is also evident that he does not wrestle with absence–presence of the deceased, his account is free from the ambivalence and vivid descriptions explored above.

Selma, 78, talked in depth about how her deceased husband is 'disappearing' more and more with each passing day. Although dear to her, she says that she cannot keep him with her. She lives a lonely life and when her children and grandchildren stop by she is only allowed to talk for a limited amount of time about sad things. This is not an outspoken rule, but she detailed how they will interrupt her if she takes too long. Since her husband is categorised as a sad topic, she does not get to speak very much about him. We have already touched upon the benefits of being able to co-construct the deceased's biography (Walter, 1996) and it appears that the lack of co-construction in this case contributes to Albert's disappearance. Selma is not permitted to properly place her husband in conversations and, so to speak, weave him into the social world with the help of others. Admittedly Albert might at this point find himself somewhere between a liminal and marginal existence, but I include him in this section because of Selma's resigned tone. She truly believes that she soon will not sense his presence at all.

The deceased might end up in the margin of the lives of the living for different reasons, then. Letting go (as much as possible) can be a relief for the living if, as in Anders' case, the relationship was very demanding. Lack of storytelling, also a prominent feature in Anders' account and presumably related to the state of his family at large, can also be important. Bonds with the deceased can be both private and public (Walter, 1999) and while Selma still maintains a fragile, private bond with Albert, she struggles with the public dimensions of it. From the deceased's point of view, life in the margin means that they suffer partial social death. Guenther (2013) states that social personhood rests on relational threads that reach into the future as well as back in the past. At this juncture it does not appear as if Albert or Anders' mother will play a significant role in the lives of their grandchildren, but this might of course change. Relationships between the living and the dead are not always linear, as Valentine (2008) convincingly demonstrates.

Disruptions leading to post-mortem social death or a life in the margin

When relationships between the living are disrupted for various reasons, the bonds that provide the deceased with a social existence may be as well. Sometimes these disruptions are so profound that all intergenerational communication ceases. Martti, 65, moved with his family from Finland to Sweden at a young age and is now starting to ponder his earliest childhood. His memories are fragmented and certain things do not seem to add up. Questions regarding his and his brother's upbringing are tied into larger questions about who their parents really were and where they came from. Since his parents and older brother are all dead, he must look elsewhere for answers. He knows of a couple of cousins elsewhere in Sweden, but they 'hardly pick up the phone' and they never respond to his invitations. As Carsten (2000) asserts, the sense that one's biography begins abruptly at birth, that nothing preceded this event, can result in feelings of disconnectedness and isolation. Martti's biography begins when he arrived in Sweden at the age of six, and the longing to feel connected is evident in his account.

Because of the disruptions, both between Martti and his parents, and between their family and other relatives, Martti is unable to relate to, for instance, his grandparents. They are unknown to him, people who have not been given life or even contours in stories told by the living. They are non-persons, to use Goffman's (1959) terminology. His parents, because of their untalkative manner, are also difficult to relate to and so grant a social existence. When asked if they ever told him anything about themselves, he answered that 'I didn't know my father very well, he never spoke about his childhood, neither did my mother, there was just this silence.' In this case the deceased either suffer almost total social death, since nothing can be said about them except that they existed, or they end up in the margin. Martti's parents have not ceased to matter, but neither of them is an 'active agent' (Mulkay & Ernst, 1991, p. 178) in his life. Possibly they could be labelled passive agents, exerting their influence by remaining silent.

Christine, 32, used to cultivate a strong continuing bond with her grandfather on her mother's side. Her mother, Maria, stored a lot of his things in a room in the cellar and they regularly spent time there, listening to his old records while drinking wine and talking about old times. As the relationship between Christine and Maria became more and more strained for different reasons, the cellar sessions came to an end. Christine says that her mother has become frail and incapable of handling grief, 'it's like she capsizes whenever she thinks about her dead'. She recognises that she has changed throughout the years as well, she seldom thinks about the deceased nowadays and she describes herself as 'closed off'. Even though she is still in contact with Maria, the relational disruption meant that her grandfather became a quiet memory.

Conclusions

In this article I have shown how the deceased can achieve a social existence through continuing bonds. Continuing bonds make the lives of the deceased 'lives that *matter*' (Guenther, 2013, p. xx, italics in original); thus they escape social death. The continuing bonds presented are formed through different practices performed by the living, storytelling being the most prominent in this case. Storytelling creates a shared history (Smart, 2007) and, I would like to stress, a shared present where the deceased exist as integral parts. In this regard storytelling is vital to the construction of what Kramer (2011, p. 392) terms the 'genealogical imaginary' – a collective biography granting all parties involved a wider, social existence. Overall, continuing bonds tend to maintain the deceased's personhood, meaning that the deceased is part of a community transcending the present (Guenther, 2013).

I have also shown how the deceased sometimes end up in a liminal state (cf. Patterson, 1982), being neither present nor absent but absent-present. The absence–presence of the deceased constitutes a uniquely mixed experience for the living (Maddrell, 2013) and makes the deceased matter in some respects but not others. There are different reasons why the deceased inhabit liminality, such as lack of (shared) continuing bond practices among the living and ambivalence when it comes to whether humans have a soul. Some of the interviewees appear to practise what Henriksson (2014) terms non-relationality, which prevent them from developing a new, adapted relationality with the deceased. It might be tempting to think that non-relationality in this context is founded solely on grief, but that would be to oversimplify. People who are grieving may indeed develop a new relationality where the deceased's personality is central, as opposed to their physical absence. Paula is a good example. A liminal state grants the deceased a semi-social, capricious existence.

The dead sometimes end up in the margin of the lives of the living. Here they suffer partial post-mortem social death. Their absence is a matter of fact phenomenon and their presence, which is randomly evoked by external elements, usually brief. They do not exert direct influence anymore (cf. Mulkay & Ernst, 1991) because they are not *experienced* as particularly significant for life here and now (although they might be in various regards). To Anders, the absence of his mother is, in many ways, a nice change. Her death relieved him from his pressing obligations as a son. For Selma, on the other hand, the disappearance of her husband Albert is anything but comforting. Even though she seems to have gotten used to the idea that his presence will fade, she is still critical of how her children and grandchildren limit her opportunities to talk about him. Because they want to keep to lighter topics, she is largely deprived of the chance to place Albert in life here and now together with them (cf. Walter, 1996).

Some deceased, finally, suffer total, or almost total, social death. Sometimes they are not embedded in the lives of the living, at other times it has to do with disrupted relationships between the living. In Martti's case the most dramatic disruption was caused by his family's move from Finland to Sweden, but it is possible that the relational disruptions within the family were equally important. He is unable to form continuing bonds with his grandparents and other relatives, since he does not know anything about them. It is almost as if they had never existed.

There is, to conclude, numerous reasons why some deceased face post-mortem social death in Sweden and others do not. The shades in between post-mortem social life and death reveal fascinating aspects of human experience and relationality. The differences between these shades, both in terms of origin and consequences, could and should be investigated further. There is of course a bigger picture to consider as well. Political, economical and cultural aspects are interwoven in migration, people's access to family ground and possibilities to free themselves from the deceased. In this article such aspects are indicated but not explored.

Acknowledgments

I would like to thank Jana Kralova for sharing her knowledge about social death with me. I would also like to thank Tony Walter for support and words of wisdom. Finally, I would like to extend my gratitude to two anonymous reviewers for valuable comments.

References

af Burén, A. (2015). *Living simultaneity. On religion among semi-secular Swedes*. Stockholm: Elanders.

Bauman, Z. (1992). *Mortality, immortality and other life strategies*. Cambridge: Polity Press.

Bauman, Z. (2007). *Liquid times: Living in an age of uncertainty*. Cambridge: Polity Press.

Bennett, G., & Bennett, K. M. (2000). The presence of the dead: An empirical study. *Mortality: Promoting the Interdisciplinary Study of Death and Dying, 5*(2), 139–157.

Bromander, J. (2012). Ritualer, högtider och manifestationer. In L. Weibull, H. Oscarsson, & A. Bergström (Eds.), *I framtidens skugga* (pp. 299–307). Göteborg: SOM-institutet.

Cacho, L. M. (2012). *Social death: Racialized rightlessness and the criminalization of the unprotected*. New York: New York University Press.

Carsten, J. (2000). 'Knowing where you've come from': Ruptures and continuities of time and kinship in narratives of adoption reunions. *Journal of the Royal Anthropological Institute, 6*, 687–703.

Carsten, J. (2007). Introduction: Ghosts of memory. In J. Carsten (Ed.), *Ghost of memory. Essays on remembrance and relatedness* (pp. 1–35). Oxford: Blackwell.

Church, S. H. (2013). Digital gravescapes: Digital memorializing on Facebook. *The Information Society: An International Journal, 29*(3), 184–189.

Day, A. (2012). Extraordinary relationality: Ancestor veneration in late Euro-American society. *Nordic Journal of Religion and Society, 25*(2), 169–181.

Empson, R. (2007). Enlivened memories: Recalling absence and loss in Mongolia. In J. Carsten (Ed.), *Ghost of memory. Essays on remembrance and relatedness* (pp. 58–82). Oxford: Blackwell.

Francis, D., Kellaher, L., & Neophytou, G. (2005). *The secret cemetery*. Oxford: Berg.

Gibson, M. (2008). *Objects of the dead. Mourning and memory in everyday life*. Melbourne: Melbourne University.

Glaser, B. G., & Strauss, A. L. (1966). *Awareness of dying*. London: Weidenfeld and Nicolson.

Goffman, E. (1959). *The presentation of self in everyday life*. New York, NY: Anchor books.

Guenther, L. (2013). *Solitary confinement. Social death and its afterlives*. Minneapolis: University of Minnesota Press.

Hallam, E., & Hockey, J. (2001). *Death, memory and material culture*. London: Berg.

Hallam, E., Hockey, J., & Howarth, G. (1999). *Beyond the body: Death and social identity*. London: Routledge.

Hammersley, M. (2008). *Questioning qualitative inquiry. Critical essays*. London: Sage.

Henriksson, A. (2014). *Organising intimacy. Exploring heterosexual singledoms at Swedish singles activities*. Karlstad: Karlstad University Studies.

Jamieson, L., & Simpson, R. (2013). *Living alone. Globalization, identity and belonging*. London: Palgrave Macmillan.

Klass, D. (1997). The deceased child in the psychic and social worlds of bereaved parents during the resolution of grief. *Death Studies, 21*(2), 147–176.

Klass, D., & Goss, R. (1999). Spiritual bonds to the dead in a cross-cultural and historical perspective: Comparative religion and modern grief. *Death Studies, 23*(6), 547–567.

Klass, D., Silverman, P. R., & Nickman, S. L. (Eds.). (1996). *Continuing bonds: New understandings of grief*. Abingdon: Taylor & Francis.

Klass, D., & Walter, T. (2001). Processes of grieving: How bonds are continued. In M. Stroebe, R. Hansson, W. Stroebe, & H. Schut (Eds.), *Handbook of bereavement research* (pp. 431–448). Washington, DC: American Psychological Association.

Kramer, A. (2011). Kinship, affinity and connectedness: Exploring the role of genealogy in personal lives. *Sociology, 45*(3), 379–395.

Maddrell, A. (2013). Living with the deceased: Absence, presence and absence-presence. *Cultural Geographies, 20*(4), 501–522.

Mitchell, M. (2007). Constructing immortality: The role of the dead in everyday life. In M. Mitchell (Ed.), *Remember me. Constructing immortality. Beliefs on immortality, life, and death* (pp. 1–18). London: Routledge.

Mulkay, M., & Ernst, J. (1991). The changing profile of social death. *European Journal of Sociology, 32*, 172–172.

Patterson, H. O. (1982). *Slavery and social death: A comparative study*. London: Harvard University Press.

Pitcher, G. (1984). The misfortunes of the dead. *American Philosophical Quarterly, 21*, 183–188.

Scarre, G. (2012). Speaking of the dead. *Mortality: Promoting the Interdisciplinary Study of Death and Dying, 17*(1), 36–50.

SOCIAL DEATH

SCB. (2013). Befolkningsstatistik 2012 - Hushållsstatistik. Retrieved from www.scb.se/sv_/Hitta-statistik/Statistik-efter-amne/Befolkning/Befolkningens-sammansattning/Befolkningsstatistik/25788/25795/Behallare-for-Press/367855/

Sifo. (2012). Spöken. Retrieved from http://www.tns-sifo.se/rapporter-undersokningar/senaste-under sokningarna/2012/spoeken

Sjödin, U. (2003). The paranormal in Swedish religiosity. In G. Davie, P. Heelas, & L. Woodhead (Eds.), *Predicting religion. Christian, secular and alternative futures* (pp. 203–213). Farnham: Ashgate.

Smart, C. (2007). *Personal life*. Cambridge: Polity Press.

Sudnow, D. (1967). *Passing on*. Englewood Cliffs, NJ: Prentice Hall.

Thompson, S. K. (2002). *Sampling* (2nd ed.). New York, NY: Wiley.

Turner, V. W. (1969). *The ritual process: Structure and anti-structure*. London: Routledge and Kegan Paul.

Unruh, D. R. (1983). Death and personal history: Strategies of identity preservation. *Social Problems, 30*, 340–351.

Valentine, C. (2008). *Bereavement narratives: Continuing bonds in the twenty-first century*. London: Routledge.

Vickio, C. J. (1999). Together in spirit: Keeping our relationships alive when loved ones die. *Death Studies, 23*, 161–175.

Wallis, J. (2001). Continuing bonds: Relationships between the living and the dead within contemporary spiritualism. *Mortality: Promoting the Interdisciplinary Study of Death and Dying, 6*(2), 127–145.

Walter, T. (1996). A new model of grief: Bereavement and biography. *Mortality: Promoting the Interdisciplinary Study of Death and Dying, 1*, 7–25.

Walter, T. (1999). *On bereavement. The culture of grief*. Buckingham: Open University Press.

Walter, T. (2012). Why different countries manage death differently: A comparative analysis of modern urban societies. *The British Journal of Sociology, 63*(1), 123–145.

Willander, E. (2014). *What counts as religion in sociology? The problem of religiosity in sociological methodology*. Uppsala: Uppsala University.

World Values Studies. (2010). Retrieved from http://www.worldvaluessurvey.org/WVSContents.jsp

Yalom, I. D. (2007). *Staring at the sun. Overcoming the terror of death*. Hoboken: Wiley.

To resist or to embrace social death? Photographs of couples on Romanian gravestones

Adela Toplean

Faculty of Letters, University of Bucharest, Romania, Bucharest, Romania

> This paper examines how a small-scale Transylvanian community uses the traditional practice of family photographs on gravestones to deal with survivors' social degradation. This practice can both affirm social death and mitigate it, depending on the survivor's will and ability to make an extra-effort to restore the tie with the deceased. Although substantial religious commitment is not necessary to engage in this practice, tie maintenance results from a serious engagement in mutual identity support and collective memory-making, with obvious spiritual overtones.

1. Introduction

'When two people marry, each one has to accept that one of them will die before the other', writes Madeleine L'Engle in the foreword of Lewis' (2009) book *A grief observed* (p. 9). As far as this paper is concerned, such acceptance implies the awareness of a probable degradation of the survivor's social life.

This article discusses the contemporary practice of engraving family photographs on gravestones, in a small Romanian Transylvanian village, Vinerea, focusing on cases when only one of the spouses is dead. I aim to analyse the connection between this practice and the survivor's experience of social deterioration. Does it cause it or alleviate it?

As this practice has been around since photography evolved to a point where anyone could afford it, it is tempting to assume that today's practices continue a traditional pattern. All traditional Transylvanian grave practices have been essentially religious, implying specific views on life and death, grief, membership in faith communities and hope for a reunited family in the other world. How substantial is this continuity in Vinerea? Does an enduring practice reflect the enduring importance of traditional meanings of losing a spouse? Or is this a modern initiative of progressively gaining control over the marital bond (Moss & Moss, 1985) without calling for specific domestic or public religious rituals? Or what about a third, 'fatal' way of looking at a photograph and seeing, as Barthes (1982, p. 14) wrote, 'Death in person', hence ruling out the possibility of successfully alleviating the prospect of the survivor's biological demise?

To address these questions, I will first discuss religion and religiosity in contemporary Romania. Some communities, including Vinerea, did not experience drastic religious restrictions

SOCIAL DEATH

during communism, which probably discouraged post-communist religious revivals. Aiming to identify whether there has been a gradual loss of dogmatic faith in this village, and if such loss is reflected in my informants' views on the couple photographs on gravestones, I will briefly consider certain historical circumstances. I will look only at factors directly impacting my topic, even though they are part of a complex picture with greater social consequences. I use Verdery's (1983, 1991, 1999) works on Romania's religious and political life during and after communism, together with younger scholarly voices and newspaper articles, to show that, after 1989, the end of official atheism did not necessarily lead to religious revival (Preda, 2011, p. 327).

I will then go on to discuss my informants' views of the photographs. To see how memory is constructed through photography, I will appeal to two philosophers and a theologian: Barthes (1982) on the photographs of his deceased mother; Ricœur (2001) on memory, history and forgetfulness (to honour the memory of his wife Simone); Lewis (2009) on grieving his wife. I use Susan Sontag's (1973/2005, 2003) two books for general interpretation of photography. In explaining how the tie is maintained after the loss of a spouse, I rely on Moss and Moss' (1985) analysis of the post-mortem persistence of the marital bond in the USA, as well as on Walter (1999) and Klass, Silverman, and Nickman (1996).

2. Religion in contemporary Romania

In 1989, after the communist collapse, the Romanian Orthodox Church (ROC) entered the new era with a credibility problem and an inability to operate in the new (media-obsessed) public sphere (Preda, 2011, p. 337). The Church had two kinds of members: 'fundamentalists of mystical and pro-Moscow orientation' (Verdery, 1999, p. 73), and more secularised believers. Although there have been constraints on church activities during communism, religion was not banned. The state even paid priests a salary. However, 'forty years without serious religious education produced nominal churchgoers who no longer know their own Orthodox religion' (p. 72).

A distinction between religiosity[1] and religion is imperative. According to Gallup's Religiosity Index (WIN-Gallup International, 2012, p. 9), 89% of Romanians described themselves as 'religious persons'. However, in 2013, trust in ROC crashed to its lowest level (Pantazi, 2013) for four years: only 66% of Romanians – compared to over 80% in previous years – found the Church reliable. A decrease in trust has been shown for Patriarch Daniel as well (Pantazi, 2013).

I argue that Romanians' religiosity can no longer be un-problematically linked to institutional religion. Studies in several western societies suggest that non-regular churchgoers see themselves as 'religious' even though they are 'secular Christians' (McAndrew & Voas, 2011; Voas & Day, 2010). Between an active churchgoer and an atheist 'the gamut of intermediate positions greatly widens: many people drop out of active practice while still declaring themselves as belonging to some confession, or believing in God' (Taylor, 2007, pp. 513, 514). 'It is more useful to view the religious and not religious as extremes, between which one finds many kinds of fuzzy religiosity' (Voas & Day, 2010, p. 1).

Why is 'fuzzy religiosity' not taken into consideration in studies of contemporary Romania? Romanians may have started their quest for direct experiences of the sacred by, among others, modifying traditional rites and old witchcraft (Bănică, 2014; Curseu, 2013) or embracing brand-new wellness techniques (Toplean, 2015).

An apparent counter-argument to an increasingly fuzzy religiosity is the steady increase in church attendance (Stahl & Venbrux, 2011, p. 145), especially in Bucharest. But one should note that in 2012 alone, over 20,000 people from poorer parts of the country moved to the capital looking for work (Mihai, 2012); they were more vulnerable financially and thus more prone to traditional religious behaviour (Norris & Inglehart, 2011, p. 3; Pargament, 1997). Patriarch Daniel contributed a great deal to urban religious bursts. He gained notoriety for bringing media visibility to

SOCIAL DEATH

ROC,[2] but also for encouraging massive religious processions and breathing new life into the cult of relics (Stahl & Venbrux, 2011, pp. 146, 147; Verdery, 1999, p. 73). For this and for other reasons, ROC's impact in the public sphere became overestimated (Preda, 2011, p. 399) and some found little justification for its recent decrease in trust. But ROC had to face numerous accusations of financial and moral compromise, of either having pro-Russia tendencies or fuelling extreme right-wing policies, and, overall, promoting an anti-West agenda (Manolescu, 2011, p. 363; Stan & Turcescu, 2007, pp. 86–89, pp. 200–208; Thedrel, 2008; Verdery, 1991, pp. 61–63; 1999, p. 73). Also, ROC has always been more or less directly involved in electoral campaigns (Stan & Turcescu, 2007, pp. 201), and its 2014 support for the left-wing presidential candidate Victor Ponta (T. D., 2014) has damaged its image even more among the pro-liberal and pro-EU voters who enabled the ethnic German ex-mayor of Sibiu, Klaus Johannis, to become Romania's first Lutheran president (Leustean, 2014). After that, the voices of pro-European right-wing Christian Orthodox intellectuals have become increasingly critical of ROC's lack of interest in ecumenical policies and Euro-Atlanticism.

In response to ROC's recent decrease in trust, the Patriarch's spokesman said: 'our churches are full' (Pantazi, 2013). True, the churches are full, and the queues to touch the relics have not become shorter.[3] Meanwhile, Bucharest is also the place where popular vegan celebrities have contributed to serious declines in vaccination rates: a 20% drop, from 2013 to 2014 (Mixich, 2015a, 2015b).

This is not to deny the importance of traditional ritual practice, but to acknowledge that not all post-communist spiritual enthusiasm unconditionally comes from traditional sources, and that Romanians' religiosity needs a larger explanatory context (Heelas, 2008; Tacey, 2004). There may be more 'sacred' focal points to consider.

3. Vinerea

Today, there are few in Vinerea identifying with religions other than Eastern Orthodoxy. However, the name of the village itself – Vilkani/Wolkani – was first mentioned in 1330 in relation to two Catholic priests (Popa, 2009, p. 177), and around the same period the Saxons started a church still in evidence at the beginning of the twentieth century (p. 180). Later, after the Saxons left during the sixteenth century reforms, the church served a small community of Greek-Catholics.[4] By the end of the sixteenth century, when Eastern Orthodoxy gain an individuality of its own (Dumitran, 2004, p. 127), an Orthodox church was erected in the heart of the graveyard that served as my research fieldwork site. Now renovated, it is one of two Orthodox churches hosting a crowded Easter Service. During usual Sunday services, however, no more than twenty people attend.

With a social structure that encouraged religious pluralism, Transylvania has for centuries been a melting pot where toleration has been greater than elsewhere (Dumitran, 2004). Vinerea's gymnasial school was called the Mixed Romanian School and it was (and is) 'strategically' located between the two churches of the village, sharing a wall with the graveyard. A woman remembers being a sixth grader in the late 1980s and being asked by her music teacher to 'cross the street' and help the church choir sing the Prohod (Requiem for the Dead) on Easter Friday. 'Of course we knew it was "wrong", but it was Easter. It was an exception.'

During communism, the village was prosperous and the school was famous for its teachers and eminent students. Most villagers worked in two factories in the nearby town: Cugir Weapon Factory,[5] and a giant Mechanical Factory founded in the eighteenth century. If the average salary in the 1980s was around 2800 lei/month, a simple worker in Cugir's factories could earn 6000 lei/month. Most villagers sent their children to good schools, soon becoming 'grandfathers of "gentlemen"' (Verdery, 1983, introduction).

SOCIAL DEATH

After the communist collapse, the two factories collapsed as well, many became unemployed, and younger workers went abroad or left for larger cities. In time, various entrepreneurs (Mercedes Benz included) bought sections of the old factories, and suddenly there was a great demand for skilled workers. Also, many have now returned from abroad and started small businesses.

One may conclude that good education, little religious constraint and a mentality historically associated with cultural pluralism did not favour religious revivals. With a general decrease in trust in ROC and no new infusion of spirituality, most villagers were left in the inertia of old Communist ways with little emotional commitment to traditional religious practices.

4. The fieldwork

As, on average, 200 persons visit Vinerea's churchyard during Easter Friday, it was a suitable time to conduct semi-structured, in-depth interviews. Twenty interviews were conducted: 9 with older men and women (7 between 60 and 70-years-old, and 2 over 70) who have already had their photograph engraved on the gravestone, 6 with younger men (between 70 and 22-years-old) who never considered using such photos, and 5 short semi-structured interviews with people attending graves of family members. Eight of the 9 informants over 60 paid regular visits to the grave (three or more times a month with no clear rituals, except for the visit itself), the rest only visiting the grave a couple of times a year, around important Orthodox celebrations. All interviews were audio recorded with a smartphone; the in-depth interviews were done during the day when the graves were being taken care of, while the short ones were done during the evening celebration. Participant observation was adopted during the day, and naturalistic observation during the evening.

4.1. *Dead or alive?*

It was Easter Friday, in 2013, the day of mourning for all the dead, according to Orthodox tradition. People all over the country returned to their birthplace to be close to their dear ones. The ancestors are missed, remembered, brought back.

'I guess I'll be buried next to him' a 63-year-old lady commented monotonously while gazing at the marble gravestone with her husband's and her own name engraved on it. There was a black-and-white photograph lit by a faint solar-powered candle, showing a young woman seated and a young man standing next to her, with his hand on her right elbow. 'He died fifteen years ago, he was a good husband' she said in the same flat voice. 'Liver cancer.' Her words were words of neither hope nor despair. If Marasco and Shuff (2010, p. 5) are right and all grief is about 'being left', this woman did not seem to feel left behind; she might have even thought she was a little bit gone already. In Barthes' (1982, p. 96) words, 'every photograph is this catastrophe', it shows a defeat of Time 'that is dead and that is going to die'. The flatness in her voice suggested that the bad has already happened. She never remarried for reasons she did not explain, but she did admit that he would have wanted her to do so. In a less-than-five-minute stroll on the cemetery's main alley, she told me her story – her *life* story, the only story able to prepare, justify and offer a horizon of interpretation for her death story. Both stories maintained – prospectively and retrospectively (Butler, 1971) – a meaningful relationship with her loved one (Walter, 1996, 1999, pp. 70–72). The initial despair and the self-verdict ('I'll be buried next to him') was corrected: her husband's reaction to this and that would have been this and that (see also Unruh, 1983, p. 340). Moss and Moss (1985) were right: the memory of the dead reinforces the identity of the living precisely because the deceased becomes the internal referee validating the widow(er)'s behaviour. But Lewis (2009, pp. 45–46) was also right: 'I should soon be using "what H. would

SOCIAL DEATH

have liked" as an instrument of domestic tyranny, with her supposed likings becoming a thinner and thinner disguise for my own.' The interplay of identities, and the overlap of statuses (see also Silverman & Klass, 1996, p. 19) are complex, confusing even. At last, it is never clear whose social death – the deceased's or the survivor's – is resisted.

And then suddenly, 'I feel like I don't know what to tell you'. But she did tell a great deal: she tried to escape her initial self-verdict of being dead and alive at the same time by telling her life story. She ended up embarrassed by her own aplomb.

4.2. *Continuing bonds*

As the evening advances, the picture becomes breath-taking. Candles are lit for the souls of the dead, an incandescent sea of light, burning like lava. Photographs are taken at every step: people take pictures of each other, they photograph themselves near the tombs they visit, they photograph old friends or neighbours met on the darkening alleys, they take photographs of the solemn procession re-enacting the Way of the Cross, symbolically built in wood and flowers and placed in the middle of the old church. As Sontag (2003) noted, since cameras were invented, 'photography has kept company with death' (p. 24). The object brought before the lens is, inevitably, 'a memento of the vanished past and the dear departed' (p. 24). There is a frenetic use of cameras and smartphones, flashlights competing with candles, a global, all-embracing remembrance, as if the crowds are here to document the show of some Jesus Christ 'Superstar' and his 'entourage'. Nothing suggests 'traditional' except the graveyard itself.

'Why are you here, dressed like that?' I ask the middle-aged lady proudly wearing a traditional costume.

> I came from Montreal, I come every year because my folks are buried here. My mother is too old to make the journey so I come here and light a candle for my grandparents. The costume is so lovely, I borrowed it for this occasion ... To feel close to my people. And to have something to show to my mother back home. She would love to see me dressed like this, standing next to the grave, next to her parents, my grandparents, she was so excited for me coming here, for days, it was all she talked about.

She points at the photograph:

> My grandmother was 95 when she died, I remember her well, but never met my grandfather. We only have a few pictures of him. But I do have a cousin who looks exactly like him in this picture. You couldn't tell the difference. Isn't that amazing?

The details one has always missed in the real person, suddenly appear clear on the photographed face (Barthes, 1982, p. 103). Seeking resemblance with other living family members (Moss & Moss, 1985, p. 199) is an at-hand strategy to maintain the connection when there are no specific expectations for an otherworldly family gathering. A visual detail is enough to make one reach back to one's ancestors, a shared reason to connect over generations, a permanent reminder of collective identity that draws the attention, as Ricœur (2001) noted, to collective memory (p. 118). There is nothing strictly individual about one's memories, because every memory is created and maintained by one's relationship with others within a social framework (Unruh, 1983). One's cousin has one's grandfather features, and one wears a traditional costume so that one's mother can rejoice in the resemblance: everybody is a part of one and the same story, and revealing one's origins is soothing. However, Barthes (1982) adds, 'the future disturbs us' (p. 105) all the more.

If Moss and Moss' (1985) perspective is essentially positive, suggesting that the dead are remembered in accordance with survivors' wishes, at the deeper level one gets a bad feeling:

SOCIAL DEATH

the more soothing the past in which we recognise our lineage, the greater the future danger. I fear the moment when I personally will no longer have eyes to see the photograph, and no longer have a memory of my own to remember my dead. One hovers between a sense of connectedness, and a subversive, traumatic feeling of loneliness and uncertainty.

The camera clicked, again and again. As I watched her taking new pictures of old pictures, it was hard to tell whether those new photographs helped the survivors resist social death. Photographs may 'create a sense of presence' (Moss & Moss, 1985, p. 198) and preserve a social identity for the dead, but photographs also predict and anticipate an absence: *your* absence. Every picture we take is an anticipation of loss. The moment the camera clicks, an absence (and, by that absence, death itself) is acknowledged.

Asked why she already had her picture on a tombstone, a 45-year-old lady admitted: 'It's a bit silly, isn't it? It's not like I'm dead. Actually, it's for practical reasons. We've ordered the stone and we wanted it to look finished.' The middle-aged lady made sure nobody looked for serious death hints when seeing their shared tombstone. Her social demise was out of the question; her biological death, ever further away. When the dead one (your spouse) and the dead-to-be (you) are brought together, you look at the picture and either see 'Death in person' (Barthes, 1982, p. 14), or a life-preserving device. It all depends on the angle and the lightning.

Which view is the 'true' view? Both, perhaps. At the 'end' of her husband's death, her own death is inscribed. 'Between the two, nothing more than the waiting' (Barthes, 1982, p. 93). Which makes me return to the opening quote of this paper: the one who survives expects a process of social degradation. Social dying is part of the 'existential protocol' of almost all modern-aged individuals. Between the death of your spouse and your own death there is some distance that needs to be travelled. One travels with the thought of death, when the body is weak and the day-to-day social interactions are fewer (Cumming & Henry, 1961; Shilling, 1993).

My informant invoked 'practical' reasons for displaying the family photograph, initiating a call for normality – this is what couples do; they do normal things, they take everyday decisions, they think practically about things, such as getting a good spot for their tomb. As long as one stays pragmatic and focused, one stays safe.

A 63-year-old former midwife has made me aware that the need for *ad-sanctos* burials is still around (Ariès, 1991, p. 33).

> Grief? No.(...) life goes on. But in the end I'll lie next to him again. We bought this grave together, we were chasing this spot since our mid-40s. We wanted to be closer to the church. (...) I don't even remember myself grieving ... It's been so long ago, but I do dream about him. Just the usual things, like entering the kitchen, asking for soup.

I would stress here the irrepressible need to preserve the intimacy with the dead (Moss & Moss, 1985, p. 201). It is the kind of intimacy that continues long after the grief fades, it has no pathological overtones (Silverman & Klass, 1996) and, according to Moss and Moss, it is one of the five persistent themes[6] that secures the bond after one is gone. Intimacy is supporting and comforting for all people, old or young, modern or traditional. The little everyday things people do together, 'the habitual patterns' (Moss & Moss, 1985, p. 201), are tools for fighting loneliness (Lewis 2009, p. 132). A feeling of belonging to a 'team' is enforced: if one loved soup when alive, one will love soup after dying, for as long as the surviving partner will live to remember it.

4.3. *Coming home*

When asked the same question (why is he already 'there', on a tombstone?), a 61-year-old man answers:

SOCIAL DEATH

> When I'll die, I'll go next to her. So why two pictures? We weren't strangers. Also, I want my grand-children to come to the grave and say look at my grandma and grandpa young and beautiful! They only knew us old and sick, it's nice to have a beautiful photo at the grave. For everyone to see. (…) It's the same photo I have on the TV set. One in the house, one in the cemetery.

It was when Barthes (1982, p. 94) looked at the photograph of his parents together that he realised that the love they shared would disappear when he, the son who testified for it, disappeared. A photograph of a couple contains as many deaths as pairs of eyes looking at it with care and concern. Commenting on Ricœur's approach of intersubjectivity and communal identity, Leichter (2012) writes: 'the transfer of the sense of selfhood from one to another carries with it an affective dimension' (p. 118). Along with the emotional attachment, there is an additional cognitive process (Silverman & Klass, 1996) stimulating connectedness within an actual (present) social context . In this sense, a photograph of the couple also contains the antidote to social dying.

The 61-year-old man and his deceased wife were anything but strangers. And we, looking at the picture, are no strangers either. We see youth in that photograph, we bond with it and, by that, we bond with *reality*. This, Sontag (2003, p. 26) writes, is the main duty of photography: to bear witness to the real. In this sense, the duty of the viewer is to *remember* (Ricœur, 2001, pp. 17, 18) a precedent reality. Remembering connects past, present and future, making one responsible to – and for – the dead. This is to say that the past is 'not over and done with' (Leichter, 2012, p. 124). Here is the point where Ricœur's phenomenology of memory and the new (continuing bonds) model of grief meet. 'Memory revitalises the past in the present' (Moss & Moss, 1985, p. 197) and thus, ideally, all social deaths have an antidote because she who has lost someone and he who is left behind are *presently* engaged in reciprocal identity support. We, strangers, confirm the mutuality, working on the collective memory of the next generation.

My informant mentions two pictures – one in the house, one in the graveyard.

Moss and Moss (1985) explain how a sense of home resembles a sense of shared identity. The homey space (p. 204) is the arena where the past is recalled and re-enacted, and Vinerea's traditional graveyard easily becomes an extension of home for villagers who have known it forever (cf Francis, Kellaher, & Neophytou, 2005). Moreover, the space around one's gravestone stirs a sense of commitment: it is this public yet familiar place where common identity is fulfilled, where subjectivity meets collectivity, where past meets present and therefore it is the place whence social death can be efficiently resisted. Although public, it is claimed as 'recoverable' and made to function as a new arena for intimate commitment; it is an extension of the house precisely because you and your dead occupy it. Visiting one's own gravestone is more a prolongation of commitment than a (traditional) ritual (Moss & Moss, 1985, p. 203).

4.4. *Going public*

As the survivor's identity depends on the deceased spouse's identity (Moss & Moss, 1985, p. 204), the survivor is concerned to gain a sense of control over that public, 'exposed' space. What role do others play in this process? What is the benefit of making an intimate photograph public? The 61-year-old man laughs when asked whether the photograph on the TV-set is different from the public one.

> Sure it's different. One shows that you've lived together and the other one that you're alright with letting people know that you had a good life together and that of course you don't plan to re-marry, haha.

People want to tell others about the good fight they fought. Remarrying is not an option once you decide 'to go public' (see also Walter, 1999, p. 20). A set of expectations, a way 'to do it' is put out there. The value of the marital bond remains intact, as the tie is supported culturally (Moss & Moss, 1985, p. 199). The social network is expected to reinforce the tie. I argue that the survivor's identity not only depends on the deceased spouse's identity, but also *on the public validation of the tie*. And perhaps this is what it takes for the survivor to efficiently resist social death.

What do others see in family photographs? A young woman answered 'Well, those people were here. And they were together.' The referentiality is neither subtle, nor questionable. It speaks about the reality of that bond which is not to be shadowed by sophisticated games of interpretation. Dismissing all knowledge, as Barthes (1982, p. 50) suggests, all you can say is that 'the photograph's essence is to ratify what it represents' (p. 85). The fact that one of the spouses is no longer alive is less important than the certainty of the couple.

If Taylor (2007, p. 141) stressed that one's identity and values are shaped though mutual recognition within a community, it is obvious why a photograph on a gravestone is more 'efficient' in preventing the survivor's social degradation than the photograph on the TV-set. We publicly recognise the certainty of a marital bond. If social death means to significantly minimise the social ties of the widow/er (Mulkay & Ernst, 1991), finding a public horizon for exposing the tie is vital. It is about bringing one's own death-style and life-style to the public scene, making the pattern recognisable and even *approved* by others. A subjective pattern is projected in the objectifying horizon of the public debate, forcing its way out, towards a shared social reality and, implicitly, towards collective memory. This is the point where individualism meets and collides with community (Walter, 1999, p. 21).

One of my youngest respondents, a 17-year-old, thinks that such photographs hold a *savoir-vivre* of some kind, a shield against loneliness. They stir 'a sense of home as I know it from my old man's stories, when he was a boy my age'.

> Hard to believe my grandparents were really young. When I see their faces here I'm thinking: it was a nice custom. It was all about the family. Today is all about ourselves. You can't use a photograph of you and your girlfriend, if you have one hehe. What are the chances to end up with her, you know what I mean?

Young people realise they belong to a different cultural set of narratives and existential structures than the pictured spouses. What do they actually understand from these pictures?

Using Husserl's concept of 'pairing', Ricœur (2001) explains the transfer of the sense of selfhood from one individual to another in the form of an associative chain (Leichter, 2012, p. 118) driven by an affective force. Two or more egos are brought together, and the associations extend across time, circumscribing the historical field of experience (p. 119). Through temporal distance, new connections and meaningful possibilities are emphasised. One generation can connect to another. Living people replace the dead ones, and each individual death reverberates publicly across the family (Moss & Moss, 1985, p. 200) and in the succession of generations. I no longer am able to understand commitment the way my grandfather did, but I am symbolically engaged in that past experience as long as I am here at the tombstone, trying to make sense of this practice. After all, my grandfather could be my *alter ego*.

The 'strangers' could see a valuable, even sacred exemplariness in these photographs, explaining their lasting importance. 'The old ones' somehow managed 'to do it better'. 'They' were luckier and less lonely than we are today. But whenever 'we' becomes 'them', something in the identity of the community gets distorted. There is a loss of social evidence of continuity (Hervieu-Léger, 2000) which shows that natural family goes through profound changes (Walter, 1999, pp. 73, 74). It is not clear whether the young

SOCIAL DEATH

ones can – by default – prevent the social degradation of the old ones. In order for this to happen, one needs to 'transform a past that is beyond one's control into a past for which we are responsible' (Leichter, 2012, p. 121).

4.5. *Modes of religiosity*

Looking at a photograph could make one ask together with Lewis (2009, p. 65): 'In what place is she at the present time?'. Indeed, this is the question. If one would only know where she is, one would finally know that the continuation of the bond is justified, thus one's social death is postponed, suspended even.

My oldest respondent was a 77-year-old retired Maths teacher. Does she believe she is going to meet her husband again? 'It doesn't matter for me as long as I will lie next to him.'

> Soon none of us will be alone. A couple of weeks before he died in '83 he said to me 'I don't want you to bury me in my best suit, it'll just get ruined. Give it to our son; but I want you to be buried in your ivory blue dress, the one that you wore at the wedding of your cousin. I liked you best in that dress. If you will be lying next to me, I want you to wear that dress. And if I'll ever meet you, I want you to wear that dress.'

Does she believe in an afterlife? 'I don't know.' She will, however, wear her blue dress even if it is too tight. She will wear it, 'just in case'. 'I hope he's at peace, forgiven. I know I did.'

A male teacher whose wife lost the battle with cancer observed: 'Poor M.! I feel less lonely when I look at this photograph. It's me who's not dead and it's her who died, one dead, one alive.' Is there a sense of connection to each other?

> I don't know, is there? (...) Who knows what's going to happen after we die? Of course the priest says we're going to meet, bla-bla. People who really believe in these things don't need a picture to remind them they will meet again. But we don't know. And that picture never lies.

A picture never lies, indeed. A reunited family? Lewis (2009, p. 67) was right, 'it rings false'. My informant 'chooses' the photograph which promises nothing. It is 'a token of absence' (Sontag, 2005, p. 12), anticipates loss and melts down all prospective hopes. Actually, a picture is without future and without culture (Barthes, 1982, pp. 89, 90). But is it also 'without' religion?

In Romanian Orthodox tradition, the materiality of visual objects – from iconographic representations to simple photos – is important for re-enforcing devotion (Firea, 2007; Stahl, 2013, p. 99; Stahl & Venbrux, 2011, p. 155). A picture of the sick retains enough of her real presence to justify, bringing it into contact with the relics and to hope for a cure (Stahl & Venbrux, 2011, p. 154). Perhaps unbelievably so, one's photograph is a material part of one's self. Traditionally, spiritual power goes to and from a visual object, which makes it either 'charged' with the sacred, or a beneficiary of the sacred touch. Sontag (2005) believes that a trace of this magic is universal. It is manifested 'in our reluctance to tear up or throw away the photograph of a loved one, especially of someone dead' (p. 125). Barthes (1982) admits there is a magic impulse making one exclaim: 'She's really there! At last, there she is!' (p. 99). This visual object not only gives the memories a certain substance, but also, for all those 'fuzzy' reasons, could stir a sacred thrill.

As far as my informants were concerned, formal religious commitment was not a necessary condition for engaging in this practice. If the priest is right and spouses are going to meet again, one does not need a photograph to be reminded of the good news. The crisis in the authority of the priesthood is, Hervieu-Léger (2000) thinks, the 'corollary of the distance each of the faithful feels entitled to set between a norm imposed from outside and the authenticity of personal experience'

(p. 132). But the photograph, as an emergent memory object (Richardson, 2014, p. 66), speaks truthfully. And it is authentic. Otherwise how could one feel less lonely just by looking at it?

There could be magic in the photograph, but what kind of 'magic'? I argue that modern or traditional, churchgoers or not, people feel motivated to preserve – perhaps religiously – some kind of togetherness. 'The urge for reunion' (Moss & Moss, 1985, p. 199) is omnipresent and could justify a belief in the afterlife, but also could justify the persistence of commitment, intimacy, identity support, family feeling and caring. This urge builds hope (Davies, 2005, p. 115), 'manipulates' expectations and handles a double fear, from 'both sides' of the fence: that of the unknown, and that of being left alone. I suspect here a subjective belief pattern, a 'fuzzy' feeling of devotion to something or someone. Sacred awe? Interpersonal connection? Both?

My informants feel no need to assure me they believe in an afterlife, but they did make a personal evaluation of the situation. What I could detect was a will to control the bond and thus to 'correct' a situation that may have otherwise favoured social dying. They do not want to be left behind and they do not want to pass away. What they consciously or unconsciously do is to modulate the 'we'. The dynamics of sustained attachment is so tight, the discourse on continuing bonds is so ambivalent, it is often difficult to tell whose social death is actually in focus, and what triggers the wish to resist it.

Ricœur's (2001) 'eschatology of memory' is of use here. One forgets, and at the same time one does not forget. An eschatological representation of the past brings *forgiveness* in focus. Forgiveness is where memory, history, and forgetfulness meet. Unlike grief that shackles one to the past, forgiving is always present. If forgetting is a 'lazy' post-grief status, forgiving is active and (arguably) religious (Ricœur, 2001, p. 590). Unlike promises, Ricœur (2001) notes, forgiveness cannot be institutionalised successfully (p. 591).

I would argue that tie maintenance through public family photographs could be a way of 'institutionalising' forgiveness. Moreover, forgiveness could be the sixth feature needed for the persistence of the bond, beside the five mentioned by Moss and Moss (1985). Through commitment, intimacy, family feeling, identity support, caring, *and* forgiveness ('I hope he is forgiven', 'Poor M.!'), one shows an active emotional engagement in the bond that can prevent the survivor's social degradation.

Even though my informants do not call on dogmatic religion to deal with their loss, the need for public validation of the photograph is based on tradition. And so is the appeal to the memory chain. Hervieu-Léger (2000), in the Durkheimian line, re-explains that religion lies *in* collective memory. If one chooses to fight social death at a biosocial level through social and cultural attachments to family and community rather than at a transcendental level through religious practices (Vigilant & Williamson, 2003, p. 3), does not that suggest – still – a spiritual agenda based on an experiential dimension of belief, triggered by the aforementioned urge for reunion? Regardless of the way one responds to loss, there is a certain *shared* quality of the effort required for maintaining the bond that mobilises every spiritual resource available, especially in persons that have lost their emotional commitment to established, ritual-based ways of grieving. It may also preserve the 'supernatural' virtues of such public photographs.

5. Conclusions

I resume here the relevant points of this article.

(a) We are probably looking in the Vinerea graveyard at a practice of continuing bonds that can both affirm the survivor's social death and mitigate it. Usually, an extra-effort is made

SOCIAL DEATH

to restore and control the tie, and to correct one's own and others' expectations accordingly.

(b) There is an interplay between public and private space that helps the survivor achieve a sense of intimacy with the dead even outside the home. On the one hand, the graveyard becomes an extension of home, so the survivor can claim the space around the gravestone as an intimate context for re-enforcing the couple's identity. On the other hand, the photograph is public, therefore waiting to be validated, putting the survivor in the position actively to "correct" her status and find ways to remain socially relevant with the help from both the community and the deceased spouse. The tie maintenance would be less efficient without the public display of the photograph.

(c) A decrease in dogmatic religious references when explaining the tie is to be noted. However, a sense of religious connectedness is not excluded, but it would need further investigation into what spirituality actually mean for these people.

(d) By suggesting forgiveness and acceptance as a sixth feature explaining the persistence of the marital tie – additional to the five suggested by Moss and Moss (1985) – I see tie maintenance as restorative, with spiritual and psychological overtones and hence an active shield against the process of social dying.

What remains unanswered is whether such corrective effort is by default successful. This has not been clear from my informants' confessions. Death may give a true measure of a togetherness's worth, but when commitment fails to manifest vigorously enough, one is perhaps left alone, exclaiming together with Barthes (1982): 'if only someone in the photographs were looking at me!' (p. 111).

Notes

1. Glock's (1973) model of religious commitment (belief, experience, knowledge, practice) is usually invoked when one attempts to measure religiosity through surveys.
2. Basilica Press Center, Basilica News Agency, http://www.basilica.ro.
3. One has to consider the political and spiritual importance of the veneration of remains in a broader context. The same pattern can be found in Balkans, the Mediterranean area and the Middle East (Håland, 2008, 2010, pp. 184, 185).
4. On how this hybrid church took shape in the 17th century's Transylvania (see: Stan & Turcescu, 2007, pp. 91, 92; Verdery, 1985, pp. 87, 107, 108, 1999, pp. 60–65, 74).
5. Before 1989, Romania was in the top ten for weapon exports, and Cugir's factory was one of the largest.
6. Together with caring, family feeling, commitment and identity support.

References

Ariès, P. (1991). *The hour of our death*. (H. Weaver, Trans.). Oxford: Oxford University Press. (Original work published 1977).

Bănică, M. (2014). *Nevoia de miracol. Fenomenul pelerinajelor în România contemporană* [The need for miracles. The pilgrimage phenomenon in contemporary Romania]. Iași: Polirom.

SOCIAL DEATH

Barthes, R. (1982). *Camera lucida: Reflections on photography.* (R. Howard, Trans.). New York, NY: Hill and Wang.

Butler, R. N. (1971). The life review: An interpretation of reminiscence in the aged. In R. Kanstenbaum (Ed.), *New thoughts on old age* (3rd ed., pp. 265–280). New York, NY: Springer Science + Business Media.

Cumming, E., & Henry, W. E. (Eds.). (1961). *Growing old: The process of disengagement.* New York, NY: Basic Books.

Curseu, I. P. (2013). *Magie si vrajitorie in cultura romana. Istorie, literatura, mentalitati* [Magic and witchcraft in Romanian culture. History, literature, mentalities]. Iasi: Polirom.

Davies, D. J. (2005). *A brief history of death.* Oxford: Blackwell.

Dumitran, A. (2004). *Religie ortodoxa – Religie reformata. Ipostaze ale identitatii confesionale a romanilor din Transilvania in secolele XVI–XVII [Orthodox religion – Protestant reformation. About confessional identities among Romanians in Transylvania during 16th and 17th centuries].* Cluj-Napoca: Nereamia Napocae.

Firea, C. (2007). Art and its context. Late medieval Transylvanian altarpieces in their original setting. *New Europe College GE-NEC Program,* 2004–2007, 319–359. Retrieved from http://www.nec.ro/pdfs/publications/ge-nec/2004–2007/CIPRIAN_FIREA.pdf

Francis, D., Kellaher, L., & Neophytou, G. (2005) *The secret cemetery.* Oxford: Berg.

Glock, Ch. Y. (1973). *Religion in sociological perspective: Essays in the empirical study of religion.* Belmont, CA: Wadsworth.

Håland, E. J. (2008). Greek women and death, ancient and modern: A comparative analysis. In E. J. Håland (Ed.). *Women, pain and death: Rituals and everyday life on the margins of Europe and beyond* (pp. 34–63). Cambridge: Cambridge Scholars Publishing.

Håland, E. J. (2010). Emotion and identity in connection with Greek death-cult, modern and ancient. *Etnološka istraživanja,* 16, 183–214, 393:291, 291.213:159.9, 159.942:29

Heelas, P. (2008). *Spiritualities of life: New age romanticism and consumptive capitalism.* Oxford: Blackwell.

Hervieu-Léger, D. (2000). *Religion as a chain of memory.* (S. Lee, Trans.). New Brunswick, NJ: Rutgers University Press.

Klass, D., Silverman, P. R., & Nickman, S. L. (Eds). (1996). *Continuing bonds: New understandings of grief.* Bristol, PA: Taylor & Francis.

Leichter, D. J. (2012). Collective identity and collective memory in the philosophy of Paul Ricœur. *Etudes Ricœuriennes,* 3(1), 114–131.

Leustean, L. (2014, November 18). A Romanian religious revolution: The orthodox church and the 2014 presidential election [blog post]. *Transatlantic Academy.* Retrieved from http://www.transatlanticacademy.org/node/742

Lewis, C. S. (2009). *A grief observed* [E-reader version]. New York, NY: Harper Collins.

Manolescu, A. (2011). Democratia pluralista: o sansa pentru desecularizarea religiei? [Pluralistic democracy: A chance to de-secularise religion?]. In C. Ungureanu (Ed.), *Religia in democratie* (pp. 356–378). Iasi: Polirom.

Marasco, R., & Shuff, B. (2010). *About grief: Insights, setbacks, grace notes, taboos.* Chicago, IL: Ivan R. Dee.

Mc.Andrew, S., & Voas, D. (2011). Measuring religiosity using surveys. *Survey Question Bank: Topic Overview* 4. Retrieved from http://surveynet.ac.uk/sqb/topics/religion/sqb_religion_mcandrew_voas.pdf

Mihai, A. (2012, August 17). Harta migratiei din judetele Romaniei. Din ce regiuni vin cei mai multi romani in Bucuresti [Migration map from Romanian districts. Where do most Bucharest immigrants come from?]. *Ziarul financiar.* Retrieved from: http://www.zf.ro/special/harta-migratiei-din-judetele-romaniei-din-ce-regiuni-vin-cei-mai-multi-romani-in-bucuresti-9953257

Mixich, V. (2015a, March 21). Cifre alarmante privind vaccinarea. [Alarming numbers concerning vaccination]. *HotNews.* Retrieved from http://www.hotnews.ro/stiri-esential-19701622-cifre-ingrijoratoare-privind-vaccinarea-bucuresti-rata-vaccinarii-ror-scazut-anul-trecut-pana-78–3-fata-97–4–2013.htm

Mixich, V. (2015b, April 27). Criza vaccinarii in Romania [The vaccination crisis in Romania]. *HotNews.* Retrieved from: http://www.hotnews.ro/stiri-esential-20017860-criza-vaccinarii-romania-cat-poate-impune-statul-cat-pot-refuza-parintii.htm

Moss, M. S., & Moss, S. Z. (1985). Some aspects of the elderly widow(er)s persistent tie with the deceased spouse. *Omega,* 15(3), 195–206.

Mulkay, M., & Ernst, J. (1991). The changing profile of social death. *Archives Europeennes De Sociologie, 32*(1), 172–196.

Norris, P., & Inglehart, R. (2011). *Sacred and secular religion and politics worldwide* (2nd ed.). New York, NY: Cambridge University Press.

Pantazi, R. (2013, February 14). Increderea in Biserica Orthodoxa Romana este la cel mai scazut nivel din ultimii 4 ani – Sondaj CCSB [The trust in the Romanian Orthodox Church, at its lowest level in the last four years – CCSB Survey]. *HotNews*. Retrieved from: http://www.hotnews.ro/stiri-esential-14226636-increderea-biserica-ortodoxa-romana-este-cel-mai-scazut-nivel-din-ultimii-4-ani-sondaj-ccsb-care-sunt-explicatiile.htm

Pargament, K. I. (1997). *The psychology of religion and coping. Theory, research, practice*. New York, NY: The Guilford Press.

Popa, C. I. (2009). Un monument medieval disparut: biserica sasilor din Vinerea (judetul Alba) [A disappeared medieval dwelling: The church of the Saxons in Vinerea (Alba district)]. *NEMVS, IV*(7–8), 176–188.

Preda, R. (2011). Ortodoxia si democratia postcomunista. Cazul romanesc [Orthodox faith and post-communist democracy. The Romanian case]. In C. Ungureanu (Ed.), *Religia in democratie* (pp. 326–356). Iasi: Polirom.

Richardson, Th. (2014). Spousal bereavement in later life: A material culture perspective. *Mortality, 19*(1), 61–79.

Ricœur, P. (2001). *Memoria, istoria, uitarea* [Memory, history, forgetting] (I. & M. Gyurcsik, Trans.). Timisoara: Amarcord. (Original work published in 2000).

Shilling, C. (1993). *The body and social theory*. London: Sage.

Silverman, P., & Klass, D. (1996). Introduction: What's the problem? In D. Klass, P. R. Silverman, & S. L. Nickman (Eds.), *Continuing bonds* (pp. 3–27). Bristol, PA: Taylor & Francis.

Sontag, S. (2003). *Regarding the pain of others*. New York, NY: Picador/Farrar, Straus and Giroux.

Sontag, S. (1973/2005). *On photography* (e-Book version). New York, NY: Rosettabooks.

Stahl, I. (2013). Getting in touch with the saints in contemporary Romania. In *Balkanskaya kartin mira sub specie pyati chelovecheskih shuvstv. Balkanskie chetniya 12. Tezisyi i materialyi (pp. 99–109)*. Moscow: Russian Academy of Sciences, Institute for Slavic Studies.

Stahl, I., & Venbrux, E. (2011). Ritual multiplication: on lived religion in Bucharest. In *Jaarboek voor liturgieonderzoek (Vol. 27, pp. 139–167)*. Groningen: Instituut voor Christelijk Cultureel Erfgoed.

Stan, L., & Turcescu, L. (2007). *Religion and politics in post-communist Romania*. New York, NY: Oxford University Press.

Taylor, Ch. (2007). *A secular age*. Cambridge, MA: Harvard University Press.

T. D. (2014, November 12). Biserica Orthodoxa Romana, agent electoral al PSD [Romanian Orthodox Church does political campaign advertising for the Social Democrats]. *Revista 22*. Retrieved from: http://www.revista22.ro/biserica-ortodoxa-romana-agent-electoral-al-psd-decaderea-morala-a-bisericii-conduse-de-patriarhul-daniel-50016.html

Thedrel, A. (2008, February 2). Les projets pharaoniques de l'eglise orthodoxe a Bucharest [The pharaonic projects of the Orthodox Church in Bucharest]. *Le Figaro*. Retrieved from: http://www.lefigaro.fr/international/2008/02/01/01003–20080201ARTFIG00478-les-projets-pharaoniques-de-l-eglise-orthodoxe-a-bucarest.php

Toplean, A. (2015, September). *Eating our way out of dying. On how medical and nutritional science has once again turned us to Believers*. Paper presented at the 12th edition of Death, Dying and Disposal International Conference, Alba Iulia, Romania. Abstract available in *Book of Abstracts*, 105. Alba Iulia: Alba Iulia Press.

Tacey, D. (2004). *The spirituality revolution: The emergence of contemporary spirituality*. New York, NY: Brunner-Routledge.

Unruh, D. R. (1983). Death and personal history: Strategies of identity preservation. *Social Problems, 30*(3), 340–351. Retrieved from http://www.jstor.org/stable/800358

Verdery, K. (1983). *Transylvanian villagers: Three centuries of political, economical, and ethnic change*. Berkley, CA: University of California Press.

Verdery, K. (1991). *National ideology under socialism: Identity and cultural politics under Ceausescu's Romania*. Berkley, CA: University of California Press.

Verdery, K. (1999). *The political lives of the dead bodies: Reburial and postsocialist change*. New York, NY: Columbia University Press.

SOCIAL DEATH

Vigilant, L. G., & Williamson, J. B. (2003). Symbolic immortality and social theory: The relevance of an underutilized concept. In Clifton D. Bryant (Ed.), *Handbook of death and dying* (vol. 1, pp. 173–183). Newbury Park, CA: Sage.

Voas, D., & Day, A. (2010). Recognizing secular Christians: Toward an unexcluded middle in the study of religion. *The Association of Religion Data Archives*. Retrieved from http://www.thearda.com/rrh/papers/guidingpapers/Voas.pdf

Walter, T. (1996). A new model of grief. *Mortality, 1*, 7–25.

Walter, T. (1999). *On bereavement: The culture of grief.* Buckingham: Open University Press.

WIN-Gallup International Survey. (2012). *Global Index of Atheism and Religiosity.* Retrieved from http://www.wingia.com/web/files/news/14/file/14.pdf

(Social) Death is not the end: resisting social exclusion due to suicide

Zohar Gazit

Department of Sociology and Anthropology, The Hebrew University of Jerusalem, Jerusalem, Israel

In most studies on those bereaved by suicide – depicted in this article as 'suicide survivors' – the social stigma of suicide results in two options for survivors: to suffer ostracism or downplay public mention of the loss, thereby contributing to the deceased's social exclusion. I suggest a third alternative – that of contesting the social death inflicted upon both the deceased and their survivors. Various qualitative methods were used to analyse *Path to Life*, an Israeli association founded by bereaved families striving to redress the segregation of people who committed suicide and those who survive them. The activists use a seemingly paradoxical strategy, by which they seek to place the cause of their social death in the limelight. Through their efforts to reframe suicide from a taboo to a widespread problem deserving recognition, the organisation's activists present the deceased and their survivors as entitled to consideration and support. The proposed analysis is based on frame analysis of 'alternative death entrepreneurs' promoting unconventional perceptions and practices concerning suicide. The case study illuminates a subject seldom investigated – efforts to transform social death.

Introduction: social death following suicide

Suicide is considered a 'bad death', meaning a death deviating from the accepted norms and regulations governing the end of life (Pool, 2004, p. 963). In addition to being violent and unexpected, an act in which a person chooses to end his or her life may raise awareness of the tension between the liberty of the individual and social control (Marks, 2003, p. 309; Marra & Orru, 1991, p. 286) and undermine the monopoly over killing claimed by modern states (Baudrillard, 1976/1993, p. 175).

Accordingly, prevalent social reactions to suicide can be seen as expressions of social death, following physical demise. The shattering act is a subject of taboo that people refrain from discussing (Leenaars, 2003, p. 143). In addition, the person who committed suicide may be excluded and segregated (Hertz, 1960, p. 85), as manifested, for example, in the manner of burial (Rugg, 2000, p. 265). The deceased might be buried at the margins of a Jewish cemetery or outside its gates, a custom still practised in some cemeteries in Israel (Gonen, 1997, p. 103).

Moreover, the circumstances of death are liable to 'pollute' the bereaved family (Niehaus, 2007, p. 857) and lead them to experience social death (Mulkay, 1993, p. 33). Those bereaved by suicide – depicted in this article as 'suicide survivors' – describe social sanctions such as being avoided (Wertheimer, 1991, p. 135), not receiving support in their grief (McIntosh, 1999, p. 168), and feeling disenfranchised grief (Doka, 2002, p. 327) whereby they are deprived of 'the right' to mourn. The actual or perceived stigma attached to the family in which a suicide has occurred may lead its members to social withdrawal and seclusion (Carter & Brooks, 1991, p. 237; Dunn & Morrish-Vidners, 1987, p. 189; Saarinen et al., 2002, p. 224), as well as to silencing the tragedy (Colt, 1987, p. 14) or attempting to present a different cause of death (Pipyrou, 2014). These feelings and actions can be understood in light of social attitudes towards suicide survivors. A study conducted in Israel (Nuttman-Schwartz, Lebel, Avrami, & Volk, 2010) reveals that people bereaved by suicide are perceived by the general public as the group least entitled to state assistance, compared with families whose loss resulted from other causes.

It would appear that suicide survivors either face ostracism or downplay the tragedy, thereby contributing to their loved one's social death. However, what of those who do not remain silent about their loss and do not conform to accepted social attitudes? They have rarely been the subject of research. This article focuses on suicide survivors who have organised under the auspices of an Israeli voluntary association striving to confront social death following suicide.

Path to Life and social activity following death

Path to Life (BeShvil HaHayim) was founded in Israel, in 2000, by family members bereaved by suicide together with experts in the field of suicide research. Its declared objectives are to support bereaved families and promote suicide prevention programmes. The organisation endeavours to advance structural-social change – through legislation and state policy – and cultural change (Jasper, 1997, p. 8) regarding perceptions and attitudes towards suicide. A less-declared yet principal aim is to alter the social exclusion of people who committed suicide and those who survive them.

Many of the organisation's activities challenge Israeli society's disregard or exclusion of suicide and are directed mainly at suicide survivors. For example, gatherings are dedicated to methods of commemorating the person who died (18 November 2009), thus giving place to the loved one who is socially forgotten; websites such as the support forum that *Path to Life* has operated since 2001 ('People whose loved ones committed suicide', http://www.tapuz.co.il/forums2008/forumpage.aspx? forumid = 56) can function as commemorating arenas and a gathering place for those who experience disenfranchised grief (Klaassens & Bijlsma, 2014, p. 291). Additionally, a main activity of *Path to Life* is to operate support groups in which members can freely express their pain and grief (Pesek, 2002, p. 127).

However, limiting activities to the backstage of society may cement the suicide survivors' marginal status. Therefore *Path to Life* members challenge social exclusion by appearing in the media, holding gatherings open to the public and – every year since 2012 – organising a procession on the streets of Tel Aviv. The event was modelled after the Out of the Darkness Community Walks, which take place in the United States (see below). It resembles the commemorative processions for AIDS casualties held in several societies since the mid-1980s, a ritual that serves as a public stage on which participants can express their grief collectively and openly, as opposed to the shame and stigma which surround the death (Power, 2009, p. 265). These goals can be traced to a comment written by a member of *Path to Life* in the organisation's online support forum regarding the first procession (9 June 2012):

> For the first time in the 4 years ... during which I have been swimming in this terrible pool of bereavement, I saw people with their heads held up high, proud people, people who want their voice to be heard, their cry – our cry.

The importance of such public activities lies in making the topic of suicide socially visible and breaking the silence surrounding it.

Path to Life can be analysed as a particular organisation of the death revival movement (Walter, 1994), seeking to raise public awareness of issues that lack social and institutional responses (O'Brian, 2012, p. 643). Verberg (2006, p. 30) analyses organisations led by bereaved family members. Like *Path to Life*, these organisations offer support to families and promote reforms in death-related state policies. Moreover, in their public activities, the 'family-based social activists' refuse to accept the norm of limiting their grief to the private sphere (Verberg, 2006, p. 40). Likewise, Breen and O'Connor (2009, p. 48) present resistance activities to the dominant grief discourse, initiated by survivors of traffic fatalities who entered the political realm and established an organisation which advocated social change. Alongside the similarities, my analysis sheds light on social activity concerning suicide. *Path to Life* members deal not only with private death, in which society has less interest (Walter, 1994, p. 189), but also with a cause of death that society denounces.

AIDS activists drew attention to a marginalised cause of death. As well as the annual procession mentioned above, a prominent project has been the AIDS Memorial Quilt, which commemorates victims of the disease. By defying mainstream attitudes regarding AIDS, by giving recognition and dignity back to the deceased (Power, 2009, pp. 261, 266), these public activities can be understood as attempts to incorporate those who died into the nation's community of honoured dead (Holst-Warhaft, 2000, p. 196). The analysis I offer describes similar aspirations, yet focuses on organisational and continuous activity, rather than on special events or projects.

A few studies have mentioned the public activities of suicide survivors, given the social attitude they face (e.g. Colt, 1987; Dunne-Maxim, 1987, p. 53; Grad, Clark, Dyregrov, & Andriessen, 2004, p. 137; Oron, 2000, p. 374). However, describing the activities is not sufficient to understand how *Path to Life* attempts to alter the denunciation of people who committed suicide and those who survive them. Another lacuna the current study addresses is activity within Israeli society. According to Spencer-Thomas and Jahn (2012, p. 80), the last decade has witnessed a proliferation of activities and advocacy organisations in the United States, led by people who attempted suicide, by bereaved families, and by other groups affected by suicide. These can be seen as a social movement in the field of suicide prevention. One such activity is the Out of the Darkness Community Walks, which began in 2003 with the aim of raising funds for the American Foundation for Suicide Prevention. In 2011 there were some 230 walks, with more than 90,000 participants in 49 states (Andersson, 2014, p. 294). Andersson (2014) interviewed people whose peer or close friend committed suicide. She analyses participation in the community walks or in prevention programmes as group-based re-enfranchising strategies, counteracting grief's disenfranchisement. In Israeli society, there is much less activity of this sort, let alone a wide movement. In addition, I use a different conceptual prism of attempts to change the social death of both the person who died and the suicide survivor.

It seems that two operational measures are open to *Path to Life* activists, but each one would hinder them in achieving their goals. Public activities on the controversial issue of suicide might raise objections and lead to exclusion. Alternatively, limiting their activities to the margins of society would reduce the disapproval they might face but make it difficult to promote broad social change. Given this difficulty, I ask: How do *Path to Life* activists justify their activities in light of the potential social sanctions, and how do they defy prevailing social attitudes towards people who committed suicide and their survivors? I contend that the activists use a seemingly paradoxical strategy, by which they seek to place suicide – the cause of their social death – in the limelight.

The proposed analysis rests on frame analysis (Goffman, 1974). Framing processes are strategic efforts of groups that produce and distribute frames, that is, interpretations of reality (Snow & Benford, 1992, p. 136), meant to motivate collective action, provide legitimacy to group activities, and influence public discourse (Hipsher, 2007). I conceptualise *Path to Life* activists as 'alternative death entrepreneurs' – social actors who promote their messages via initiatives (Noakes & Johnston, 2005, p. 7). *Path to Life* activists frame suicide and dealing with suicide in a way that is designed to gain legitimacy for their activities. It entails changing their status and that of their loved ones from socially dead – segregated, avoided and forgotten – to socially alive, deserving recognition and consideration. They do so by using frames and arguments that have cultural resonance (Ferree, 2003, p. 339) and which are likely to raise less resistance and negative feedback (Coy, Woehrle, & Maney, 2008, p. 165). At the same time, in order to change the status quo, frames should include elements that challenge prevalent interpretations of reality (Gamson, 1985, p. 616). Hence, the alternative death entrepreneurs distribute frames that combine the accepted with the unaccepted, avoiding both integration into the established institutional orders and marginalisation to the periphery of political consciousness (Carroll & Ratner, 2001, p. 609).

Methodology

This paper is part of a research project which analyses and compares three social organisations in contemporary Jewish society in Israel, each seeking to advance alternatives to the hegemonic conceptions and practices regarding death (Gazit, 2015).[1] The research was approved by the Ethics Committee of the Faculty of Social Sciences at the Hebrew University of Jerusalem.

Most of the fieldwork was conducted between 2009 and 2011. Data were collected and analysed using various qualitative methods. Regarding *Path to Life*, I conducted 17 semi-structured interviews with key members. In addition, I participated in *Path to Life*'s meetings; gatherings open to the public; a lecture given by the chairman to college students; discussions in the Israeli parliament (Knesset); and a public procession held in Tel Aviv. A third source of data I used is cultural artefacts: I analysed invitations to events held by the organisation or with the participation of its members, distribution materials, the website and *Path to Life's* online support forum, its Facebook page, and appearances of its members in different websites. I analysed 77 media appearances, including interviews with the organisation's members, references to the organisation, a television documentary series in which members participated, comments that members wrote in response to articles concerning suicide, and members' letters to the editor. Additionally, I analysed TV and radio commercials the organisation produced. Another platform of activity was the Knesset: I analysed references to the organisation in reports of the Knesset's information centre, parliamentary committees' minutes in which members took part and members' letters to Knesset committees.

When analysing the data, I paid attention to symbolic aspects of collective activities (Pedriana, 2006, p. 1721), as well as rhetorical strategies used by the activists to justify their unconventional activities and challenge prevailing attitudes (Ellingson, 1995, p. 104). I organised the data according to themes. A main theme was revealed during this process, of attempts by *Path to Life* members to alter social attitudes towards people who committed suicide and the bereaved families. Alongside adopting the perspective of the research participants, I sought to offer an explanation connected to theoretical conceptualisation (Denzin, 1978, p. 61), mainly social death and framing processes, as described above. I then organised the data in light of the main theme and by doing so developed an explanatory model (Strauss & Corbin, 1990, p. 23) from the case study examined (George & McKeown, 1985, p. 24), a strategy that forms part of grounded theory (Eisenhardt & Graebner, 2007, p. 25). The explanatory model, which I verified through repeated readings of the data (Strauss & Corbin, 1990, p. 133), is composed of three different, interrelated, facets of the strategy *Path to Life* members employ in their attempts to alter social death. These include emphasising connections between suicide and socially noticeable causes of death, framing suicide as an all-encompassing threat no one is immune to, and framing

Path to Life's activities as potentially life-saving. The next three sections of the article are organised according to the components of my explanatory model.

Suicide and socially visible causes of death: from exclusion to inclusion

Different causes of death have different degrees of social prestige. The higher a cause of death is located in the socio-cultural 'death hierarchy' (Brawer Ben David, 2006), the more it is visible and publically discussed. One technique the members of *Path to Life* use to overcome their status as socially dead is to call attention to the resemblance between suicide and socially noticeable causes of death.

Demise in a traffic collision is perceived as accidental, not resulting from a deliberate decision to terminate life. Hence it is viewed less negatively than suicide and is located somewhat higher in the death hierarchy (see also Nzioka, 2000, p. 6). In light of this attitude, *Path to Life* members draw parallels between suicides and traffic collisions, so as to undermine distinctions between the two causes of death.

In the interviews I have conducted, *Path to Life* members stressed points of resemblance regarding the unexpectedness of both deaths and the guilt feelings bereaved parents may harbour in either case. When appearing in the media, references were made to the number of casualties, whereby *Path to Life* members argue that the number of people dying by their own hands is in fact higher than the number of traffic fatalities. For example, in a television documentary programme (Ben Dor, 2010), Yaron,[2] *Path to Life* chairman, said:

> … I think the numbers of those committing suicide is … higher than [those dying in] traffic collisions … but here [in the case of suicide] … there is no national authority acting to reduce … suicides and to support families whose loved ones committed suicide … this has no rational explanation, unless they want to bury this issue.

Pointing out similarities between the two causes of death, as well as an elevated risk of suicide, questions the differences in social attitudes and treatment received at the hands of the Israeli authorities. *Path to Life* members make allegations regarding the absence of a national programme to prevent suicide and to aid bereaved families, in contrast to the case of traffic collisions. They also protest against a situation in which, according to them, traffic collisions receive wide media coverage, while suicide almost never gets mentioned (Aderet, 2007). The comparison undermines the division between 'legitimate' causes of death, worthy of public attention and support, and suicide, which is neglected. It is also a plea for social acknowledgment of the difficulties suicide survivors encounter.

Another kind of death referenced by the members of *Path to Life,* related to the national context, is that occurring during mandatory military service and active service in wars. This is located at the top of the death hierarchy, is highly regarded and has a high profile in Israel's public sphere. Its centrality is manifested, amongst other things, in street names dedicated to fallen soldiers, annual remembrance days enacted by law (Azaryahu, 1995, pp. 127, 142), and commemorative monuments spread across the country (Shamir, 1996, p. 9).

Path to Life members underline connections between death in the military institution and dealing with suicide with the aim of gaining legitimacy for their activities. One approach is by imitating military modes of support to bereaved families. Miriam, a *Path to Life* management member, described to me meetings with personnel from the Ministry of Defence, in order to learn their mode of operating support groups for bereaved families. Additionally, some of the groups *Path to Life* operates are guided by professionals with prior experience of working with the Ministry of Defence. Adopting the characteristics of the support groups operating within the military establishment is meant to present *Path to Life's* activities as based on the accepted model, an isomorphism of a normative body (DiMaggio & Powell, 1983). In addition, dealing with suicide and its outcomes is framed as no different in essence from dealing with death in the national context.

Alongside making connections between their activities and highly visible military deaths, *Path to Life* activists highlight the subject of suicide in the army. Amir, who acts as a liaison between *Path to Life* and the military, argued in a media interview (Zelikovitch, 2004) that an estimated 10% of fallen soldiers in Israel died not in combat or in training accidents, but by their own hands. Other members, when appearing in the media, have emphasised the risk of committing suicide during military service. Such claims blur the distinction between deaths that are excluded and deaths that are revered. Both circumstances of death are framed as not being mutually exclusive, thus reducing the social distance between those who took their own lives and casualties of national related deaths. Holst-Warhaft (2000, p. 187) argues that the war veterans who made the decision to erect the Vietnam Veterans Memorial Wall in Washington did so with the purpose of commemorating the Americans who died in an unpopular war that most Americans would have preferred to forget. In a similar manner, *Path to Life* members draw attention to people who died in the army, but in circumstances that are marginalised. Moreover, military death is presented in a new light – one connected to a risk of suicide, pertinent to soldiers. Thus attention is drawn to the cause of death, which is framed as an untreated social problem.

Suicide as a widespread threat: from marginality to centrality

Highlighting soldiers' suicide risk can raise the issue of suicide on the public agenda. *Path to Life* members follow this course of action by framing suicide as a risk relevant to society as a whole. Family-based social activists attempt to demonstrate that their 'private' experience is in fact a 'public' issue (Verberg, 2006, p. 34). Describing their activities as addressing a collective need is a strategy that activists use to present their motivations as guided by more than mere narrow interests (Blython & Jenkins, 2012, p. 38). This presentation also pertains to modifying the status of social death.

A message advanced by *Path to Life* is that no one is immune to the risk of suicide, and that everyone might be a potential victim of the social problem they are committed to publicising (Best, 1987, p. 108). A visual manifestation of this can be found in invitations to the organisation's gatherings (e.g. 28 April 2004; 9 June 2009), showing unidentified, nameless faces, who can be any John/Jane Doe. Another example was presented in a television documentary programme (Ben Dor, 2010), in which an activist from *Path to Life* is seen giving a lecture and asking those in the audience who knew of someone who contemplated suicide, or even attempted the act, to raise their hands. Almost all hands are raised. The prevalence of the threat is stressed. Additionally, in *Path to Life's* online support forum (6 November 2003) and in appearances in the media (Nir, 2008), the members talked about 'an epidemic of suicides' in Israel and suicides as a 'national calamity', thus strengthening a perception of an all-encompassing, ubiquitous threat.

Furthermore, members use suicide statistics in a strategic way to highlight an increasing risk. According to the Ministry of Health, from the year 2000 to 2011 an annual average of 397 suicides was registered in Israel, with the overall rate of suicides slightly decreasing (Goldberger, Haklai, & Aburba, 2014). Yet, according to a *Path to Life* pamphlet distributed in 2010, about 450 people commit suicide every year, and two years later, in a radio interview (Barkai, 2012), a member claimed 550 people commit suicide annually. How can the discrepancy in the data be explained? It is assumed that official statistics concerning suicide are inaccurate due to underreporting and concealment (Timmermans, 2005, p. 322). *Path to Life* members use this assumption.

In a discussion in the Knesset (2007, March 14) David, a management member of *Path to Life*, said:

> Many people prefer not to report ... because if you report a suicide you will be buried 'outside the gates'[of the cemetery], there will be a stigma attached to you, the family will suffer ... therefore ... we do not know the actual number [of suicides] in Israel.

Questioning the credibility of the official statistics contends a higher-than-reported number of suicide casualties and an increasing risk, based on an unempirical estimation. The lack of credible data also enables members of *Path to Life* to criticise formal state policy concerning suicides. For example, Dan, the administrator of the online support forum, wrote (1 November 2008): 'Why doesn't the Ministry of Health provide reliable and updated data? ... my opinion is that this is a deliberate policy, caused by fear of dealing with public pressure to address this subject.' State authorities are thus reproached for deliberately marginalising the issue instead of giving it much needed attention.

Framing suicide risk as an all-encompassing problem transforms it from a minor social concern to a pressing issue that should be placed at the centre of public debate and preoccupation. Given the arguably wide-reaching and escalating threat, *Path to Life* members advocate a prognostic frame (Snow & Benford, 1988) involving diverse social systems to prevent suicide. A national prevention programme should include, as prescribed by the *Path to Life* website (http://www.path-to-life.org): ' ... the educational system ... police, law, religion ... politicians, and the media'.

Presenting suicide as posing a widespread threat from which no one is entirely safe also defies the social stigma attached to people who took their own lives and their survivors. A message repeated at *Path to Life*'s gatherings (8 June 2010; 7 September 2011) emphasises not only that suicide might occur in any family, but also the normality of the families in which suicides occurred. Hence, the cause of death is framed as not necessarily indicating a shortcoming in those who committed suicide or their families.

Suicide in the limelight: from social taboo to saving lives

As opposed to activists in 'consensus movements', such as *Mothers against Drunk Driving*, whose cause receives support from the community (Edwards & McCarthy, 2004, p. 623), *Path to Life*'s objectives lack social legitimacy. Attempts to highlight the issue of suicide risks clashing with both common perceptions and expert opinion that publicising suicides is likely to encourage more suicides (see Callahan, 1996; Lee, Lee, Hwang, & Stack, 2014). *Path to Life* activists confront this difficulty and seek to transform the issue of suicide from social taboo to potentially life-saving. One example is an invitation to an event the organisation held ('Can we <u>really</u> prevent suicides?' 2011, March 24) which was publicised as a ' ... conference ... which brings together professionals and family members that will say ... : Yes ... Talk about it! Talk in order to prevent'.

Another example of the organisation's efforts to present itself as life-oriented while dealing with suicide came up in an interview with the coordinator of the support groups *Path to Life* operates. She claimed that the supposedly elevated risk of suicide survivors committing suicide (McMenamy, Jordan, & Mitchell, 2008, p. 376) may be reduced by participating in a support group, in which individuals can share emotions in empathetic surroundings. As such, she argued, the group plays a part in saving lives by providing its members something to look forward to in their distress.

Furthermore, through *Path to Life* support groups, online forum support and gatherings, members are encouraged to nurture oppositional movement identities (Futrell & Simi, 2004, p. 16) that defy the conventions of silencing public discussion. A main object of the organisation is to reduce the shame and social withdrawal and motivate the members to take part in public activities. The importance of talking about suicide is stressed, and suicide survivors who 'come out of the closet' and relate their personal story receive praise for their courage. Efrat, a management member in the organisation, said at the end of a gathering (18 November 2009): 'If we will stop being ashamed ... then maybe our voice will begin to be heard ... those sitting here need to take an active part, it's beyond the support groups. We need you ... !'. The connection between public activities of suicide survivors and changing social attitudes towards them is emphasised.

A key incentive in encouraging and justifying dealing with the cause of social death, in light of potential hostility and rejection, is preventing more tragedies. This can be seen in what Dan, the administrator of *Path to Life's* online support forum, wrote (20 May 2011) regarding his sister's suicide:

> [I] ... can get angry at the 'cursed gun' she used ... [I] can get mad at [myself] ... [There's another way] ... we can choose life ... I chose to act for ... bereaved families ... I chose to act to increase the awareness of ... suicide and [act for] its prevention.

'Choosing life' by focusing on suicide may appear paradoxical at first glance. Yet, it can be understood as a means to redefine the nihilistic act of suicide as a constructive resource, which may prove beneficial to *Path to Life* members and to society (see Armour, 2003, p. 534; Rock, 1998, p. 133 for a similar claim concerning the activity of bereaved families following homicide). The invitation to participate in the organisation's public activities offers a unique opportunity to transform the seclusion, the passivity, the feelings of anger and despair following the loss, into a pursuit of a social life, in the form of activity that takes place in public and that aids in preventing more death.

Moreover, the activity is framed as socially reviving the loved one who died. A pamphlet distributed in a *Path to Life* gathering (7 September 2011) encourages members to partake in meetings at schools in which they would tell their personal story:

> ... This activity ... enables us ... to make a significant contribution to preventing tragedies of the kind we have experienced. For many of us this activity is also an important sort of commemoration of our loved ones and [gives] a feeling their death was not in vain.

In the previous section I analysed the manner in which *Path to Life* activists strategically use suicide statistics. In other contexts, a complementary strategy is used to counteract social death: sharing personal stories to negate writing off the deceased as a mere regrettable statistic (Santino, 2004, p. 370). Furthermore, commemoration through activity aimed at preventing suicide is a way to include the family member who committed suicide in a positive context (Maple, Edwards, Minichiello, & Plummer, 2013, p. 62). In the online support forum of *Path to Life* (4 February 2003), Yaron, the chairman, encourages members to view their activities as carrying out a will, left by their loved ones. Thus the family member who committed suicide is framed as playing a pivotal part in *Path to Life's* prevention efforts.

Discussion and conclusion: *Path to (social) Life*

The members of *Path to Life* struggle to unravel the silence, to overcome the marginalisation and the ostracism – those manifestations of social death resulting from suicide – as they aspire to social life. They are struggling to influence policy-makers to obtain formal support in the form of state remunerations for bereaved families, as well as for informal recognition, such as a 'right' to mourn their loss and commemorate their loved ones. This article has focused on a seemingly paradoxical activity by which the organisation's members deal intensively and publicly with the cause of their social death. Evading exposure will leave both those who died and their bereaved families marginalised. Hence, without endorsing suicide in any way, *Path to Life* members frame a certain perception of it: a cause of death that shares commonalities with other, more socially visible and tolerated causes of death; a risk that hovers above all men and women; a threat that can be prevented if discussed and attended to. These frames justify public interest in the issue, undermining the taboo and consequent social death of suicide survivors.

Social death and physical death denote different things, yet the two are also tightly connected. Some causes of death, such as suicide, may lead to social death. A different manifestation of this connection can be traced in the activities of *Path to Life*. In order to change social death, the organisation's members, as alternative death entrepreneurs, reframe physical death. By doing so, they blur accepted boundaries between death and life as well as those of Israel's prevalent socio-cultural death hierarchy.

A key strategy of *Path to Life* accentuates life, a safer and richer life, achieved through confronting suicide. Instead of causing rejection, the taboo is transformed to lure supporters and to allow the organisation access into the collective arena. A manifestation of this can be witnessed in the inner-organisational level, in messages directed to *Path to Life* members, through framing confronting suicide as an empowering resource in the lives of those willing to take part in the organisation's activities. An additional manifestation is aimed at the public. Verberg (2006, p. 28) claims that family-based social activists, in their endeavours to promote social change concerning death-related issues, leave us with a sense of despair that is rooted in the senseless death, and a sense of hope that rests with the possibility of changing the conditions which led to the tragedy. Likewise, *Path to Life* frames the current situation as carrying a wide suicide risk, yet it is not an irrevocable fate; through dealing with what the public currently would rather avoid, the threat can be diminished. By putting suicide on the agenda, the lives of those dealing with it and society at large will be rewarded. The conduct of *Path to Life* is framed as carrying a social contribution, while the cause of social death is framed as an integral part of life, not to be neglected.

In addition, the alternative death entrepreneurs challenge the death hierarchy. *Path to Life* presents itself as relevant to society as a whole. The concern for the general public and the relevance to the collective imply and resemble national death, which is considered a collective issue in Israeli society. It is yet another example of imitating characteristics of national death, but which serves to promote alternative perceptions and practices and attempts to blur the boundaries between suicide and other causes of death. Pointing out similarities and connections to more visible causes of death is meant to change the significance of suicide from a singular and differentiated death and to outline a common ground of socially accepted grief that includes people who took their own lives and suicide survivors.

This article focused on the framing activities of *Path to Life*. Further researches can examine public acceptance – or rejection – of the frames promoted by *Path to Life* and analyse whether the alternative perceptions and practices distributed by the organisation contribute to changes in the suicide discourse in Israel. A different line of inquiry can compare *Path to Life*'s activities with those of other organisations, for example associations established by family members following loss due to drug use, another stigmatised cause of death for the deceased and his family (Guy & Holloway, 2007), and expand the picture presented in this article regarding activities of bereaved families facing social denunciation and rejection.

Social death, in the aftermath of physical death, can become the starting point for activities that strive to transform this marginalised status. The tragedy cannot be undone. The consequences and implications of such marginalisation, however, are not necessarily a permanent condition inflicted upon a group but may be contested and redefined by those affected.

Acknowledgements

An early version of this article was presented at the Centre for Death & Society Conference, University of Bath, June, 2014. I wish to express my gratitude to the participants for their enriching remarks. I am especially grateful to Tony Walter for bringing to my attention the similarities between 'bad deaths' resulting from suicide and drug use. I also wish to thank the editors and two anonymous reviewers for their valuable comments. In addition, my thanks go to Shunamith Carin and to Yoav Cohen for providing insightful editorial help. This paper is part of my doctoral research. I am grateful to my supervisors, Nurit Stadler and Gad Yair, for their support throughout the project. Above all, I wish to thank the members of *Path to Life* who participated in this study, for their willingness to share with me their experiences and losses.

Disclosure statement

No potential conflict of interest was reported by the author.

Funding

The research was funded by the President Scholarship for PhD candidates at the Hebrew University of Jerusalem, The Levi Eshkol Institute for Social, Economic and Political Research in Israel, the Khayyam Zev Paltiel Endowment for an annual prize in Israel Social Policy, and the Department of Sociology and Anthropology at the Hebrew University of Jerusalem.

Notes

1. The other two organisations concern euthanasia and burial.
2. All names are pseudonyms.

References

Aderet, A. (2007, November 14). A mute cry. *nrg*. Retrieved from http://www.nrg.co.il (in Hebrew).

Andersson, T. (2014). "Nobody talks about suicide, except if they're kidding": Disenfranchised and re-enfranchised grief and coping strategies in peer suicide grievers. In J. R. Cutcliffe, J. C. Santos, P. S. Links, J. Zaheer, H. G. Harder, F. Campbell, … R. Eynan (Eds.), *Routledge international handbook of clinical suicide research* (pp. 289–297). London: Routledge.

Armour, M. (2003). Meaning making in the aftermath of homicide. *Death Studies, 27*, 519–540.

Azaryahu, M. (1995). *State cults: Celebrating independence and commemorating the fallen in Israel 1948–1956*. Be'er Sheva: Ben-Gurion University of the Negev Press (in Hebrew).

Barkai, R. (2012, October 10). Where's the fire? *Galey Tzahal*. Retrieved from http://www.youtube.com (in Hebrew).

Baudrillard, J. (1976/1993). *Symbolic exchange and death*. (I. Hamilton Grant, Trans.). London: Sage.

Ben-Dor, O. (writer & director) (2010). On guilt and responsibility [Television series episode]. In N. Maiman (Producer), *When pain is Unbearable*. Tel Aviv: Hot. Retrieved from http://www.ynet.co.il (in Hebrew).

Best, J. (1987). Rhetoric in claims-making: Constructing the missing children problem. *Social Problems, 34*, 101–121.

SOCIAL DEATH

Blython, P., & Jenkins, J. (2012). Mobilizing resistance: The Burberry workers' campaign against factory closure. *The Sociological Review*, *60*, 25–45.

Brawer Ben-David, O. (2006). Ranking deaths in Israeli society: Premature deaths and organ donation. *Mortality*, *11*, 79–98.

Breen, L. J., & O'Connor, M. (2009). Acts of resistance: Breaking the silence of grief following traffic crash fatalities. *Death Studies*, *34*, 30–53.

Callahan, J. (1996). Negative effects of a school suicide postvention program: A case example. *Crisis*, *17*, 108–115.

Carroll, W. K., & Ratner, R. S. (2001). Sustaining oppositional cultures in "post-socialist" times: A comparative study of three social movement organizations. *Sociology*, *35*, 605–629.

Carter, B. F., & Brooks, A. (1991). Child and adolescent survivors of suicide. In A. A. Leenaars (Ed.), *Life span perspectives of suicide: Time-lines in the suicide process* (pp. 231–258). New York, NY: Plenum Press.

Colt, G. H. (1987). The history of the suicide survivor: The mark of Cain. In E. J. Dunne, J. L. McIntosh, & K. Dunne-Maxim (Eds.), *Suicide and its aftermath: Understanding and counseling the survivors* (pp. 3–18). New York, NY: W. W. Norton.

Coy, P. G., Woehrle, L. M., & Maney, G. M. (2008). Discursive legacies: The U.S. peace movement and "support the troops". *Social Problems*, *55*, 161–189.

Denzin, N. K. (1978). The research act. In J. G. Manis & B. N. Meltzer (Eds.), *A reader in social psychology* (pp. 58–68). Boston, MA: Allyn & Bacon.

DiMaggio, P. J., & Powell, W. W. (1983). The iron cage revisited: Institutional isomorphism and collective rationality in organizational fields. *American Sociological Review*, *48*, 147–160.

Doka, K. J. (2002). How we die: Stigmatized death and disenfranchised grief. In K. J. Doka (Ed.), *Disenfranchised grief: New directions, challenges, and strategies for practice* (pp. 323–336). Champaign, IL: Research Press.

Dunn, R. G., & Morrish-Vidners, D. (1987). The psychological and social experience of suicide survivors. *Omega*, *18*, 175–215.

Dunne-Maxim, K. (1987). Survivors and the media: Pitfalls and potential. In E. J. Dunne, J. L. McIntosh, & K. Dunne-Maxim (Eds.), *Suicide and its aftermath: Understanding and counseling the survivors* (pp. 45–56). New York, NY: W. W. Norton.

Edwards, B., & McCarthy, J. D. (2004). Strategy matters: The contingent value of social capital in the survival of local social movement organizations. *Social Forces*, *83*, 621–651.

Eisenhardt, K. M., & Graebner, M. E. (2007). Theory building from cases: Opportunities and challenges. *Academy of Management Journal*, *50*, 25–32.

Ellingson, S. (1995). Understanding the dialectic of discourse and collective action: Public debate and rioting in Antebellum Cincinnati. *American Journal of Sociology*, *101*, 100–144.

Ferree, M. M. (2003). Resonance and radicalism: Feminist framing in the abortion debates of the United States and Germany. *American Journal of Sociology*, *109*, 304–344.

Futrell, R., & Simi, P. (2004). Free spaces, collective identity, and the persistence of U.S. white power activism. *Social Problems*, *51*, 16–42.

Gamson, W. A. (1985). Goffman's legacy to political sociology. *Theory and Society*, *14*, 605–622.

Gazit, Z. (2015). Struggle to the death: Promoting alternative perceptions and practices concerning death in Israeli society (Unpublished doctoral dissertation). The Hebrew University of Jerusalem, Jerusalem (in Hebrew).

George, A. L., & McKeown, T. J. (1985). Case studies and theories of organizational decision making. In R. F. Coulam & R. A. Smith (Eds.), *Advances in information processing in organizations*, Vol. 2 (pp. 21–58). Greenwich, CT: JAI Press.

Goffman, E. (1974). *Frame analysis: An essay on the organization of experience*. New York, NY: Harper & Row.

Goldberger, N., Haklai, Z., & Aburba, M. (2014). *Suicidality in Israel: Suicides 1981–2011, Suicide attempts 2004–2012*. Jerusalem: Information and computer services, information department, Ministry of Health (in Hebrew).

Gonen, A. (1997). Choosing the right place of rest: The socio-cultural geography of a Jewish cemetery in Jerusalem. In H. Brodsky (Ed.), *Land and community: Geography in Jewish studies* (pp. 87–104). Bethesda, MD: University Press of Maryland.

Grad, O. T., Clark, S., Dyregrov, K., & Andriessen K. (2004). What helps and what hinders the process of surviving the suicide of somebody close. *Crisis*, *25*, 134–139.

Guy, P., & Holloway, M. (2007). Drug-related deaths and the "special deaths" of late modernity. *Sociology*, *41*, 83–96.

SOCIAL DEATH

Hertz, R. (1960). *Death and the right hand*. (R. Needham & C. Needham, Trans.). London: Cohen and West.

Hipsher, P. L. (2007). Heretical social movement organizations and their framing strategies. *Sociological Inquiry, 77*, 241–263.

Holst-Warhaft, G. (2000). *The cue for passion: Grief and its political uses*. Cambridge, MA: Harvard University Press.

Jasper, J. M. (1997). *The art of moral protest: Culture, biography, and creativity in social movements*. Chicago, IL: The University of Chicago Press.

Klaassens, M., & Bijlsma, M. J. (2014). New places of remembrance: Individual web memorials in the Netherlands. *Death Studies, 38*, 283–293.

Knesset, Protocol 372 of the Finance committee meeting (2007, March 14). Financing a national program to confront suicide. Retrieved from https://www.knesset.gov.il (in Hebrew).

Lee, J., Lee, W. Y., Hwang, J. S., & Stack, S. J. (2014). To what extent does the reporting behavior of the media regarding a celebrity suicide influence subsequent suicides in South Korea? *Suicide and Life-Threatening Behavior, 44*, 457–472.

Leenaars, A. A. (2003). Suicide and human rights: A suicidologist's perspective. *Health and Human Rights, 6*(2), 128–148.

Maple, M., Edwards, H. E., Minichiello, V., & Plummer, D. (2013). Still part of the family: The importance of physical, emotional and spiritual memorial places and spaces for parents bereaved through the suicide death of their son or daughter. *Mortality, 18*, 54–71.

Marks, A. H. (2003). Historical suicide. In C. D. Bryant (Ed.), *Handbook of death & dying* (pp. 309–318). Thousand Oaks, CA: Sage.

Marra, R., & Orru, M. (1991). Social images of suicide. *The British Journal of Sociology, 42*, 273–288.

McIntosh, J. L. (1999). Research on survivors of suicide. In M. Stimming & M. Stimming (Eds.), *Before their time: Adult children's experiences of parental suicide* (pp. 157–180). Philadelphia, PA: Temple University Press.

McMenamy, J., Jordan, J. R., & Mitchell, A. M. (2008). What do suicide survivors tell us they need? Results of a pilot study. *Suicide and Life-Threatening Behavior, 38*, 375–389.

Mulkay, M. (1993). Social death in Britain. In D. Clark (Ed.), *The sociology of death: Theory, culture, practice* (pp. 31–49). Oxford: Blackwell Publishers/The Sociological Review.

Niehaus, I. (2007). Death before dying: Understanding AIDS stigma in the South African Lowveld. *Journal of Southern African Studies, 33*, 845–860.

Nir, H. (2008, December 12). Family relations. *Yediot Ashdod, Ashkelon, HaDarom*, Retrieved from http://www.img2.tapuz.co.il (in Hebrew).

Noakes, J. A., & Johnston, H. (2005). Frames of protest: A road map to a perspective. In H. Johnston & J. A. Noakes (Eds.), *Frames of protest: Social movements and the framing perspective* (pp. 1–29). New York, NY: Rowman & Littlefield.

Nuttman-Shwartz, O., Lebel, U., Avrami, S., & Volk, N. (2010). Perceptions of suicide and their impact on policy, discourse and welfare. *European Journal of Social Work, 13*, 375–392.

Nzioka, C. (2000). The social meanings of death from HIV/AIDS: An African interpretative view. *Culture, Health & Sexuality, 2*, 1–14.

O'Brian, T. (2012). Environmental protest in New Zealand (1997–2010). *The British Journal of Sociology, 63*, 641–661.

Oron, I. (2000). A support group for parents whose children committed suicide: From professional guidance to self help. *Society & Welfare, 20*(3), 361–383 (in Hebrew).

Pedriana, N. (2006). From protective to equal treatment: Legal processes and transformation of the women's movement in the 1960s. *American Journal of Sociology, 111*, 1718–1761.

Pesek, E. M. (2002). The role of support groups in disenfranchised grief. In K. J. Doka (Ed.), *Disenfranchised grief: New directions, challenges, and strategies for practice* (pp. 127–133). Champaign, IL: Research Press.

Pipyrou, S. (2014). Narrating death: Affective reworking of suicide in rural Greece. *Social Anthropology, 22*, 189–199.

Pool, R. (2004). "You're not going to dehydrate mom, are you?": Euthanasia, versterving, and good death in the Netherlands. *Social Science and Medicine, 58*, 955–966.

Power, J. (2009). Rites of belonging: Grief, memorial and social action. *Health Sociology Review, 18*, 260–272.

Rock, P. E. (1998). *After homicide: Practical and political responses to bereavement*. Oxford: Clarendon Press.

Rugg, J. (2000). Defining the place of burial: What makes a cemetery a cemetery? *Mortality, 5*, 259–275.

Saarinen, P., Irmeli, H., Jukka, L., Johannes, L., Jouko K., & Viinamaki, H. (2002). Mental health and social isolation among survivors ten years after a suicide in the family: A case-control study. *Archives of Suicide Research, 6*, 221–226.

Santino, J. (2004). Performative commemoratives, the personal, and the public: Spontaneous shrines, emergent ritual, and the field of folklore (AFS Presidential Plenary Address, 2003). *Journal of American Folklore, 117*, 363–372.

Shamir, I. (1996). *Commemoration and remembrance: Israel's way of molding its collective memory patterns*. Tel Aviv: Am Oved (in Hebrew).

Snow, D. A., & Benford, R. D. (1988). Ideology, frame resonance, and participant mobilization. *International Social Movement Research, 1*, 197–217.

Snow, D. A., & Benford, R. D. (1992). Master frames and cycles of protest. In A. D. Morris & C. M. Mueller (Eds.), *Frontiers in social movement theory* (pp. 133–155). New Haven and London: Yale University Press.

Spencer-Thomas, S., & Jahn, D. R. (2012). Tracking a movement: US milestones in suicide prevention. *Suicide and Life-Threatening Behavior, 42*, 78–85.

Strauss, A., & Corbin, J. (1990). *Basics of qualitative research*. Newbery Park, CA: Sage.

Timmermans, S. (2005). Suicide determination and the professional authority of medical examiners. *American Sociological Review, 70*, 311–333.

Verberg, N. (2006). Family-based social activism: Rethinking the social role of families. *Socialist Studies/ Études Socialistes, 2*(1), 23–46.

Walter, T. (1994). *The revival of death*. London: Routledge.

Wertheimer, A. (1991). *A special scar: The experiences of people bereaved by suicide*. London and New York: Tavistock/Routledge.

Zelikovitch, M. (2004, September 5). Jewish men commit suicide 3 times more than Arab men. *Ynet*. Retrieved from http://www.ynet.co.il (in Hebrew).

The agency of dead musicians

Lisa McCormick

Department of Sociology, University of Edinburgh, Edinburgh, UK

A long-standing theme in the sociology of the arts is the sacralisation of art in modern society, but an underexplored aspect of this process is how death shapes artistic creation and appreciation. This paper approaches this issue through an examination of the cult of the dead composer in classical music. After considering the cultural logic and effect of musical sainthood, I discuss how composers are venerated; commemorative rites, such as anniversary programming, provide a phenomenological connection between the living and the dead, while physical remains and relic-like objects carry messages from beyond the grave that can be usurped or amplified by political projects. By comparing the fetishisation of the dead diva with the composer cult, I explain why performers who continue to be admired posthumously still do not achieve the same exalted status as composers.

I was first introduced to the concept of sainthood at age eight in religion class at a Catholic primary school in Western Canada. Our teacher offered an age-appropriate explanation: saints are special people remembered long after their death for doing extraordinary things who are now in Heaven with God because of their good works. I considered this for a moment, and raised my hand when she asked for examples. 'J.S. Bach!' I declared, confident I had found someone who fit all the criteria. This composer commanded total respect from my music teachers; my cello lessons on his compositions took on a reverential tone because, they told me, I was finally playing 'real music'. For years, I was teased for this innocent mistake, and not only because I had failed to understand why a Lutheran was ineligible for this distinction.

In retrospect and from a sociological perspective, it is unsurprising that a child would assume that Bach was a saint. The sacralisation of art in modern society is a standard theme in the sociology of the arts; nowhere is this more obvious than in Bourdieu's (1984, [1983] 1993) now-orthodox perspective which analyses the 'consecration' of artists in the field of cultural production and the 'charismatic ideology' which shrouds the social determinants of good taste. However, the established approaches for emphasising the religious dimension of artistic creation and appreciation have distracted from the importance of death in shaping these cultural processes. In this paper, I aim to address this oversight in two ways: by examining the cult of the dead composer and by unearthing the role of (im)mortality in the sociology of the arts.

SOCIAL DEATH

My initial task is to establish that classical music is dominated by the dead, which will not come as news to either musicologists or classical music devotees. Neither would opera fans raise an eyebrow, death being a central theme in many of the most celebrated operas (e.g. *Lucia di Lammermoor, La Bohème, Tosca* or anything by Wagner). However, the omnipresence of death in classical music culture makes it that much more surprising that it has never been adequately theorised. I will treat posthumous influence as a form of musical agency; drawing from Heinich (1996), I first discuss the 'Beethoven effect' and the social process through which composers are raised to musical sainthood. In the next section, I explore the commemorative rituals through which living musicians connect with the dead and explain the appeal of anniversary programming using Schütz's (1951) phenomenology. While sound is of primary importance in musical culture, material objects also play an important role in composer cults; in the following section, Chopin's heart serves as the main example of how political events further infuse musical relics with meaning. To conclude, I compare the fetishisation of dead divas to composer cults in order to explain why only composers achieve immortality.

The ghosts of composers past

Classical music has been criticised for being locked in a 'museum culture' (Boulez, 1986; Burkholder, 1983), and it is easy to understand why. The design of instruments and performance venues has changed little in over one 100 years. Advanced musical training takes place in aptly named conservatories where teachers proudly trace their pedagogical lineages through several generations of bygone masters. But the most striking respect in which the present musical culture is haunted by the past is the prominence of dead composers. As Nettl (1995) observed, the rhetoric used in music schools would leave an outsider at a loss in distinguishing the quick from the dead; students speak of 'going to hear Beethoven' in the same way they describe going to hear a friend perform a recital. At lessons and in rehearsals, aspiring musicians are trained to submit to the authority of the score and to strive for 'authenticity'. These maxims are dogmatic among specialists in historically informed performance, but they are not exclusive to them. Living musicians pursue the intentions of dead composers, often zealously, and sometimes at the expense of contemporary aesthetic standards. If believing in the composer's better judgement were not already enough to sustain it, the ethics of this approach to interpretation have also been defended by declaring the performance intentions of dead composers a special case of 'our obligation to comply, where we can, with the wishes and intentions of the dead' which 'has its source in our duty to refrain from injuring the interests of others' (Kivy, 1993, p. 114).

Given that composer's performance intentions carry such weight, it is not surprising that conservatories, chamber ensembles, and symphony orchestras often invite contemporary composers to participate in the final stages of preparing their music for performance. Kanno (2012) argues that even in this situation, the norm of the deceased composer prevails. The partitioning of creativity in Western classical music is so institutionalised that performers approach pieces 'as if the composer is dead', discerning what they can from a score handed to them as a *fait accompli*. The 'last-minute rehearsal' with contemporary composers, an all-too-common scenario in the professional world, provides only enough time to uncover unintentional divergences from their intentions; furthermore, resolving them interactively would demand a different kind of creativity from the one cultivated in conservatories which depends on the composer's deceased status.

Concertgoers are so accustomed to hearing centuries-old music that they are often startled when someone sitting in the concert hall is acknowledged as the composer of a piece on that evening's programme. But it was not always so. Weber (1984, p. 175) has traced the 'epochal change in the balance between the past and the present in Western musical life' that occurred between 1700 and 1870. Traditionally, the majority of music performed was by living musicians who were also composers, and turnover in the repertoire was so regular that a composer's works were rarely heard after his death. Exceptions only began to appear in the eighteenth century; Lully's operas were regularly heard at the Académie royale de musique (Paris Opera) for almost a century after his death in 1687 (Rosow, 1989), and Handel's music grew in popularity in England, Europe, and America after he died in 1759 (Harris, 1992). The watershed came after the turn of the nineteenth century, when concerts were devoted to the symphonic and chamber works of Haydn, Mozart and Beethoven; essayists began calling this music "Classical," conservatories made it into a curriculum, and critics defined it as the highest musical authority' (Weber, 1984, p. 175). These gradually became the norm, and by the 1870s, concert programmes were dominated by the works of deceased masters.

Elsewhere, Weber (1994) provides statistical evidence gleaned from concert programmes to show increasing preference for the music of the past. The most striking example is the *Gesellschaft der Musikfreunde* in Vienna. Between 1815 and 1825, 77% of the works performed were by living composers; this proportion diminished to 53% between 1838 and 1848, and then to 18% in the ten seasons after 1849. A similar trend is found in solo recitals and professional orchestras across Europe. Weber (1994, p. 5) argues that the 'rise of the masters to musical sainthood' should be understood as an early form of mass culture fed by the commercial interests of the emerging music industry.

The respect for the deceased masters was exported beyond Europe by elites and itinerant musicians, but as Dimaggio (1982) has shown, the orchestral canon did not take root in the USA until the 1900s because it was not commercially viable; crucial for its establishment was the development of the non-profit organisational form which could insulate orchestras from commercial pressures. According to Dimaggio, organisations like the Boston Symphony Orchestra, which dedicated themselves to performing 'the classics', provide the necessary social foundation for aesthetic classification; they facilitate the process of 'sacralisation' through which selected cultural objects come to be considered as superior to others and cordoned off from those deemed mundane or vulgar.

In addition to transforming audiences' tastes, the growing preoccupation with the musical past also affected composers; they were no longer writing 'for the moment' and whatever the occasion demanded, 'but rather in competition with the musical giants of the past for posterity' (Harris, 1992, pp. 208–209). Straus (1991) argues that this 'anxiety of influence' arises from how composition is taught; studying the works of deceased masters, composers come to revere these great figures but also to be intimidated by them. Because a dialogue with the past cannot be avoided, composers must choose between incorporating and revising traditional materials in their music.

Few deceased masters cast as long a shadow as Beethoven. His posthumous influence has been summarised by Ross (2014, p. 44):

> The professional orchestra arose, in large measure, as a vehicle for the incessant performance of Beethoven's symphonies. The art of conducting emerged in its wake. The modern piano bears the imprint of his demand for a more resonant and flexible instrument. Recording technology evolved with Beethoven in mind: the first commercial $33^{1/3}$ rpm LP, in 1931, contained the Fifth Symphony and the duration of first-generation compact disks was fixed at seventy-five minutes so that the Ninth Symphony could unfurl without interruption.

And the list goes on. However, the form of posthumous musical agency that has most interested musicologists is Beethoven's effect on later generations of composers. Burnham (1995, p. xiii) confirms that his middle-period style has 'epitomized musical vitality' for nearly two centuries because it became 'the paradigm for Western compositional logic and of all the positive virtues that music can embody for humanity'. For example, Fisk (1994, p. 397) uses the opening of Beethoven's Symphony No. 5 to demonstrate the 'inner life of old music' that grows from ambiguity; Beethoven's development of musical materials sets up expectations for both the 'naïve' and the 'experienced' ear, some of which are 'met, others denied, still other changed and redirected', but all of them 'engag[ing] the ear and the mind' with the 'purpose of speaking to the heart' (p. 401).

Chopin is conventionally identified as one of the few canonical composers to have escaped Beethoven's influence by focusing on genres that Beethoven never explored, such as nocturnes and mazurkas. But even this exception has been eroded such that Chopin is brought into Beethoven's orbit. For example, Petty (1999, p. 284) argues that the B-flat minor piano sonata, a genre too closely associated with Beethoven to ignore him, is 'fertile ground for considering what it meant to Chopin to be an artist living in a world haunted by the ghost of Beethoven'; his analysis presents the famous Funeral March movement as a death scene where Chopin both puts Beethoven to rest symbolically and draws himself 'toward the past, one including Beethoven' (p. 298).

I would call this the 'Beethoven effect', a musical parallel to what Heinich (1996) terms the 'Van Gogh effect' in visual art. Heinich accomplishes an 'anthropology of admiration' by tracing the posthumous cultural construction of Van Gogh. Having died in relative obscurity, he might well have been forgotten or simply branded as a deviant because of his mental illness. But he escaped both oblivion and stigmatisation, becoming instead an object of devotion, and this destiny has done more than simply secure his place in art history; Van Gogh's legend became the archetypal model of the artist, in the sense both of an example to be imitated and of a patterned configuration of values (Heinich, 1996, p. 141). It ushered in a new order; in the place of traditional standards of artistic excellence, abnormality became highly valued, incomprehension became a recurring motif, and consecration became displaced into posterity. The 'Van Gogh effect' has not only been transferred to future generations of artists; it is also applied to those who predated him through a retrospective reinterpretation of art history.

Van Gogh's posthumous transformation occurred in six stages:

> his work was made into an enigma, his life into a legend, his fate into a scandal, his paintings were put up for sale and exhibited, and the places he went, as well as the objects he touched, were made into relics. (1996, p. 140)

The crucial element in his rise to sainthood is self-sacrifice. In biographical narratives, Van Gogh is shown to have suffered for his art; he ruined his physical and mental health, eventually making the ultimate sacrifice by taking his own life. This final gesture secured the cultural logic of martyrdom; the failure of Van Gogh's contemporaries to recognise his greatness became an injustice for which 'society' in general is blamed. Heinich suggests that pilgrimages to art museums where Van Gogh's paintings are venerated can be understood as a form of atonement to restore the asymmetry produced by the irreversibility of death.

The Beethoven legend also features suffering. His major affliction was deafness, but his manuscripts, which are littered with corrections and scribbled out passages, also provide evidence that he struggled with composing and was rarely satisfied with his work. The incomprehension motif is established through anecdotes portraying him as underappreciated in his lifetime, despite his champions' best efforts. In one famous episode from 1802, Beethoven snarls 'I do not play for such swine' having grown frustrated with the inattentive audience at a salon performance (quoted in DeNora, 2006, p. 111). His posthumous critical reception, however, praised his originality, excused his uncouth behaviour, and transformed him into 'a secular god, his shadow falling on those who came after him, and even on those who came before him' (Ross, 2014, p. 44).

SOCIAL DEATH

The popular conceptions of other musical masters are mostly variations on this theme. But rather than demonstrating how the facts of various composers' lives are made to fit this model, the next section will explore how the veneration of musical saints has become embedded in musical life.

Gone but never forgotten: commemorative musical rites

A range of actors participate in the posthumous cultural construction of the composer. The Polish pedagogue Jerzy Żurawlew established the Fryderyk Chopin International Piano Competition because he was concerned with the composer's legacy and believed that a competition could reinforce the continuity of tradition that had begun to splinter amongst the pupils of Chopin's pupils (Ekiert, 2010, p. 7). Handel serves as an even better example: John Mainwaring, an English clergyman, published a full-length biography and criticism of his music the year after Handel died (the first publication of this kind about a composer); professional and amateur ensembles, including The Academy of Ancient Music, the Concerts of Ancient Music, the Three Choirs Festival and the Handel and Haydn Society, regularly performed his music; and publishers produced and distributed special editions of his works (Harris, 1992). In 1784, the directors of the Concerts of Ancient Music also organised a commemoration, the date chosen (erroneously) to celebrate the centennial of Handel's birth on the 25th anniversary of his death. This 'novel festival', which consisted of five concerts held in Westminster Abbey and a West End entertainment palace, was of an unprecedented scale, 'captur[ing] public attention all around the Western world' (Weber, 1989).

It is ironic that such a grand commemorative spectacle would be put on for Handel who was never in danger of being forgotten. But he is the exception; the reputations of most musical masters had to be resurrected after a period of obscurity. The first composer to be 'rediscovered' is J.S. Bach, and it is a fellow composer, Mendelssohn, who is credited with reviving interest in his music by conducting a performance of the *Saint Matthew Passion*.[1] From then on, composers were frequently advocates for their predecessors: Berlioz studied and edited the music of Gluck; Vaughan-Williams participated in editing the complete works of Purcell; Saint-Saëns edited the complete works of Rameau; and Webern edited the complete works of Isaac' (Harris, 1992, p. 210). Later generations of conductors also followed Mendelssohn's example by championing previously neglected composers; for example, Leonard Bernstein endeavoured to be seen as the one who 'put Mahler on the map' by producing several recordings of his works, giving lectures and writing essays in praise of Mahler's compositional style, and placing Mahler's symphonies at the core of his programmes (Schiff, 2001).

What is striking about the Bach and the Mahler revivals is how they coincide with anniversaries; Mendelssohn conducted the Bach *Passion* on what he believed was the 100th anniversary of its first performance, while Mahler's symphonies achieved mainstream status on the centenary of his birth. Commemorative programming has since become a mainstay in musical life. The idea of the 'The Bach Year', when the anniversary of composer's birth or death is marked by an outpouring of musicological scholarship and special performances of his work, has been extended to all members of the 'classical canon' and beyond. For example, 2013 was the centenary of Benjamin Britten's birth[2] as well as Wagner and Verdi's bicentennials, which provided an excuse (if one was needed) for opera houses everywhere to stage productions of their operas; 2014 was the year to honour Gluck and Richard Strauss while in 2015, Nielsen, Sibelius and Scriabin had their turn being feted. In years not coinciding with births and deaths, outstanding compositional achievements are commemorated; Carnegie Hall marked the 45th anniversary of Terry Riley's 'In C' in 2008, while few orchestras missed the opportunity to perform Igor Stravinsky's *Rite of Spring* in 2013 to mark its 100th anniversary. Concertgoers can now easily predict whose music will dominate each new season; those seeking a more diverse musical diet must resort to promoting overlooked anniversaries or inventing new milestones (Service, 2015).

It is tempting to attribute the rise of commemorative programming to marketing forces. But while the publishing and recording industry certainly benefit from the boost in sales, it is doubtful that 'anniversarising' would have flourished to this extent if musicians and audiences did not also find it meaningful. A key to understanding the appeal of commemorative programming can be found in Schütz's (1951) phenomenological analysis of music-making, a theory developed to refute Halbwachs' (1980) theory of collective memory among musicians which emphasised notation (a visual symbolic system) in the transmission of musical thought. To displace the centrality of the text, he proposed the idea of the 'mutual tuning-in relationship', a social interaction so fundamental that it forms the precondition for the communicative process. For Schütz (1951, p. 79), marching, dancing and making love together were all examples of intersubjectivity, but he chose music-making to analyse how 'the "I" and the "Thou" are experienced by both participants as a "We" in vivid presence'.

Schütz (1951, p. 93) argued that the 'tuning in' required to make music had the effect of synchronising 'inner time' so that participants in a musical performance were 'living together through the same flux' and 'growing older together' for the duration of the musical process. These participants included the musicians who coordinated their thoughts and actions to play a piece of music, as well as the listeners who attended to these sounds, an orientation that he insisted did not depend on specialised knowledge. Another participant was the composer of the piece of music. Schütz considered both musicians and listeners as 'beholders' of music who could 'tune in' with the composer, even if this person was dead:

> Although separated by hundreds of years, the [beholder] participates with quasi simultaneity in the [composer]'s stream of consciousness by performing with him step by step the ongoing articulation of his musical thought. The beholder, thus, is united with the composer by a time dimension common to both, which is nothing other than a derived form of the vivid present shared by the partners in a genuine face-to-face relation. (Schütz, 1951, p. 90)

What makes it possible for 'beholders of music' to achieve intersubjectivity with each other and with absent or dead composers is the 'polythetical structure' of music. Schütz insists that a similar connection cannot be achieved with deceased mathematicians or authors because mathematical formulas, like sentences, can be grasped 'in a single glance' once the series of mental operations that constructed its content have been performed. In contrast, musical meaning resists such reduction. This is a difficult distinction to defend, not least because it does not reflect the compositional process of most composers; it can also be misread as a theory that reduces the performer to a mere vessel connecting the listener to the composer. Schütz, as a phenomenologist, was less concerned with these musicological issues; he sought to emphasise the temporal and intensely collaborative nature of musical *experience*. The study, rehearsal and performance of music involve unfolding its content in time 'step by step', and by experiencing its reconstitution, the 'quasi simultaneity' of the beholder's stream of consciousness with that of the composer's is re-established (Schütz, 1951, p. 91).

While any musical performance has the potential to become an act of communion in this phenomenological sense, commemorative programming organises and elevates these experiences to a ritual status, thereby shaping the 'topography of the past' (Zerubavel, 2003) that relates the special dead to each other and to the present musical community. The now-expected surge in popularity following a composer's death might be fuelled by marketing, but commemorations held long after the fact sustain a cultural dialogue about the meaning of that composer in contemporary musical life. In the next section, I will discuss how material memorials provide another opportunity for the living to connect with a world that has been lost by tuning into a message from 'beyond the grave'.

Sacred sites and musical relics

According to the church historian Angenendt (2010), the dead lost their agency and their legal status during the Enlightenment. Medieval Christians had shared with archaic religions the belief that the dead were not truly dead and that a life force remained in the corpse that must be maintained for the afterlife. While the theological leaders in the Protestant Reformation had discouraged the veneration of relics, it was medical science that eventually dealt the more serious blow to this tradition; when people became persuaded that the dead body was not just life-less but poisonous, a religious form that had continued through human history came to an abrupt end. With the church reforms of Emperor Joseph II in the eighteenth century, the only relics that remained were those that satisfied a specified standard of evidence.

Beyond the religious sphere, 'relic-like' behaviour has persisted into the modern era, especially in societies with a Catholic or Orthodox Christian heritage. The 'political religions' of Soviet communism and German National Socialism provide the most striking examples of how these early Christian cultural scripts for remembering the revered dead were transposed into the political realm (Maier, 2006). In the former case, Bolsheviks had deliberately undermined religious belief, and attacked the Orthodox Church, by opening graves and destroying shrines; but when Vladimir Ulyanov-Lenin died, political leaders reverted to the very cultic rituals they had denigrated by embalming his body and laying it to rest in a mausoleum for public veneration. In the latter case, the celebrated dead were the 16 putschists killed at the Munich *Feldherrnhalle* on 9 November 1923. At the memorial erected on the site, SS guards kept constant vigil and passers-by were expected to raise their arm in a Nazi salute; on the anniversary of the Putsch in 1935, the bodies of the martyrs were exhumed and placed in bronze sarcophagi to lie in state before being taken to the Temple of Honor where they would become the Eternal Guard (Baird, 1990, p. 59).

The diversity of cultic practices in modern Europe and beyond inspired a reconceptualisation of the relic. For Walsham (2010), relics are much more than material objects that are tied to an individual and the time or events with which he or she is associated; because the item is thought to capture the essence of the dead person, relics are ontologically distinguishable from representations or images that would merely symbolise the divine presence. Accordingly, relics can be understood to function as:

> material manifestations of the act of remembrance. They sublimate, crystallize, and perpetuate memory in the guise of physical remains, linking the past and present in a concrete and palpable way ... A kind of umbilical cord that connects the living and the celebrated dead, they carry messages from beyond the grave and provide a mnemonic ligature to a world that has been lost. (Walsham, 2010, p. 13)

Nor does this function depend on the object's uniqueness; relics and replicas do not always exist in a hostile oppositional relationship.

In the realm of classical music, a category of objects amenable to 'relichood' (Gillingham, 2010) are sculptures bearing the likeness of revered composers. In the nineteenth century, replicas of Beethoven's death mask became a standard 'part of the décor of the middle-class drawing room' (Ariès, 1981, p. 262); nowadays, they are more likely to be found in museums, tucked away in a glass case along with some of the great man's personal possessions. However, miniature

SOCIAL DEATH

busts continue to be a popular decoration in domestic and educational environments. Throughout the nineteenth century, these were manufactured in a range of materials, from pottery and stoneware to porcelain and 'Parian-ware'; they remain a standard item in music gift shops today, though they are more likely to be made out of plastic or vinyl (Hunter, 2014). While death masks connect the living with the dead by preserving imprints of the revered musician's body, the pint-sized bust of Bach perched on the local music teacher's upright piano links the past to the present in a different way; these 'bite-sized' monuments reduce the monumentality of deceased master composers to more manageable scale by offering living performers a simpler, if sometimes caricatured, version of their personality and their role in music history (Hunter, 2014).

The advantage of these relic-like objects is that they are both portable and replicable, whereas gravesites are fixed in space. For early medieval Christians, the resting places of saints became holy because their bodies were believed to hold a sacred power (Angenendt, 2010). Laqueur (2011, p. 810) argues that this belief anchored a new and consequential necro-geography; beginning in the fifth century, the 'ordinary dead' wanted to rest in or near a church where the body of the 'special dead' (a saint) was enshrined, 'protecting all the other bodies' in the vicinity 'with its aura'. This spatial arrangement of dead bodies would not be challenged until the emergence of the modern cemetery which became a 'place unto itself' (Laqueur, 2011). But even without the connection to the church, these burial grounds would come to house their own 'special dead', including revered musicians.

For example, Beethoven was interred in the cemetery at Währing and Schubert, who had been a torchbearer at Beethoven's funeral, expressed his wish the night before he died to be buried next to Beethoven.[3] Even after their remains were moved to the Zentralfriedhof in 1880, Währing was a pilgrimage site (B, 1892). However, the musical pilgrim seeking Mozart's place of rest in the churchyard of St. Marx nearby would search in vain; he was buried in a mass grave, and the memorials erected after his death could indicate only the general area where his remains are likely to be. While most graveside visits are done to offer a private tribute to the celebrated dead, Van Cliburn's musical pilgrimage was a newsworthy event. After the Texan pianist won the 1958 Tchaikovsky Competition in Moscow at the height of the cold war, he made a point of visiting Tchaikovsky's grave while on the winner's concert tour of the Soviet Union. But this was only the first stop on the pilgrimage; upon returning to the USA, he visited Sergei Rachmaninov's grave in New York to plant a Russian lilac next to it using soil taken from Tchaikovsky's grave ('All-American Virtuoso', 1958).

Revered musicians' remains have also been used as instruments of legitimation in political projects, especially in socialist counties. Bohuslav Martinů, the exiled Czech composer who died in Switzerland in 1959, was reinterred 20 years later in his birthplace, the village of Polička, despite having indicated that he did not want to return to Czechoslovakia while it remained Communist and despite the regime's initial hostility towards him; his gradual rehabilitation as an anti-fascist (if not Communist) composer culminated in the reburial ceremony where he was hailed by the Minister of Culture as 'a jewel of Czech national culture' and 'an inseparable part of our cultural heritage' (Beckerman, 2007, p. 1). Similarly, Béla Bartók left Hungary in 1940 as a protest against the influence of German fascism in his homeland and died in New York in 1945. Although he was known as a composer of 'difficult' music, the return of his remains to Communist Hungary after 43 years set off a 'publicity extravaganza' in the Hungarian media that successfully transformed him into a national hero for party hardliners and oppositional intellectuals alike, and his lavish state funeral 'mobilized the uncoerced participation of many thousands of otherwise politically disenchanted people' (Gal, 1991, p. 440).

The Polish Government's repatriation of the famous pianist and statesman Ignacy Jan Paderewski in 1992 provides an example of a reburial in a post-socialist society. When Paderewski died in the USA in 1941, President Roosevelt issued a directive for him to be buried temporarily in Arlington National Cemetery with the expectation that his remains would be returned to Poland after the war. After the installation of the communist regime, Poland twice requested for the body to be returned, once in 1947, and again in 1963. President Kennedy responded the second time by declaring that he would remain in the USA until Poland was free, a wish Paderewski had indicated in his will. While his body eventually went home, Paderewski's heart remains in in Doylestown, Pennsylvania at the Shrine of Our Lady of Czestochowa.[4] In the case of Paderewski's fellow countryman, Fryderyk Chopin, it was not his corpse that travelled back to Poland but his heart. In reviewing Pettyn's (2011) chronicle of Chopin's heart, we can observe how a composer's remains come to be seen as national treasures in the first place.[5]

On his deathbed, Chopin expressed his last wishes to those who had gathered around him. He provided specific instructions about what music should be played at his funeral, including Mozart's Requiem and the funeral march from his own sonata in B-flat minor. He also requested that an autopsy be performed after his death because he feared being buried alive (Eisler, 2003).[6] And he asked his sister, Louise, to take his heart to Warsaw: 'I know that Paskévitch would not permit you to transport my body to Warsaw, so take at least my heart' (Musielak, 2003, p. 83, n. 31, author's translation).

The heart was preserved in alcohol and encased in an urn, which Louise smuggled into Poland by hiding it under her cloak. Initially, the clergy at the Church of the Holy Cross (Kościół Świętego Krzyża) in Warsaw refused to place the urn in the upper church because Chopin was not a saint; it was stored in the catacombs for 30 years before the Parish priest agreed to have it deposited in the first pillar on the left from the nave's side. The placement of the urn was done in secret in order to avoid drawing the attention of tsarist authorities, but its location was subsequently marked with a plaque proclaiming 'here lies the heart of Frederic Chopin' along with an elaborate memorial stone bearing an inscription from the Gospel of St. Matthew (6:21): 'Where your treasure is, there your heart will be also.'

The Holy Cross memorial remained the only public monument to Chopin until a statue was unveiled in Warsaw's Royal Baths Park (Łazienki Królewskie) in 1926. It did not stand for long. When the Nazis occupied Warsaw in 1939, they destroyed the statue, and in a futile attempt to suppress nationalist sentiments, the public performance of Chopin's music was banned. The heart was nearly lost during the turmoil of the Warsaw uprising of 1944; when the violence began to approach the vicinity of the church, Schulze, a German chaplain, convinced the Holy Cross clergy to let him take it to a safe place, which is how it wound up in the care of Heinz Reinfarth, an SS officer who professed to be an admirer of Chopin's music. After the uprising was suppressed, the commander of operations in the region, Erich von dem Bach, attempted to stage an elaborate return of the urn to Polish hands for propaganda purposes, but a technical malfunction prevented the film crew from documenting the exchange. The Holy Cross priests, suspicious of this seemingly noble gesture, secretly took the urn thirty kilometres west to Milanówek for safekeeping, first at a private residence, and then on the piano in the Archbishop's private chapel. The heart was finally returned to Warsaw in 1945, on the anniversary of Chopin's death. It was taken by car on a route that had been decorated with flags; eye witness accounts describe crowds of people waiting at the capital in silence, uncovering their heads at the sight of the car, some stepping forward to toss a bouquet of flowers on the vehicle carrying the precious cargo as it passed by.

Concluding thoughts: the object of devotion

Every musical genre has its own pantheon of departed greats, some of whom are raised to musical sainthood. After John Lennon, a founding member of the Beatles, was shot, biographies that portrayed him as anything other than a prophetic figure, social activist or happy househusband were soundly denounced as blasphemous (Sherwood, 2006); Jim Morrison's grave at Père Lachaise cemetery and Elvis Presley's Graceland remain popular pilgrimage sites (Margry, 2008). However, classical music is exceptional in the degree to which deceased musicians maintain a presence in musical life, which is why it provides an ideal case for exploring the agency of the dead in the developed Western world. Composers are not the only 'special dead' worthy of commemoration in the world of classical music; performers often receive posthumous adulation as well. But this is better understood as an extension of the celebrity they experienced in their lifetime rather than as another manifestation of the 'Beethoven effect' described earlier. To clarify this difference, I will briefly examine the fetishisation of the dead diva.

In his ethnography of Argentinian opera fanatics, Benzecry (2011, p. 115) describes how even deceased vocalists are the object of an admiration so intense that it takes on a 'quasi-religious character'. The most 'literal' example he offers is the memorial service for Victoria de los Ángeles, a Spanish-American soprano, that was held a year after her death. The Catholic ceremony, which was attended by more than 300 people, concluded with a recording of the deceased singer performing Gounod's 'Ave Maria' which brought applause and shouts of 'Bravo'.

Benzecry also recounts the stubborn efforts of one group of fans to have a commemorative plaque for Claudia Muzio placed in the Teatro Colón more than three decades after her death. While many such plaques can be found at the Colón, and at every major performance venue for that matter, this small memorial suddenly became a big deal when the house director threatened to remove 'Divina' (divine) from the inscription. The timing could not have been worse; the director revealed this intention shortly before Joan Sutherland was scheduled to give her debut at the Colón singing the part of Violetta in *La Traviata,* a role that was known to be Muzio's favourite. After Sutherland's 'stormy' debut (Figueroa, 1969), the director gave into their demands, believing that the group of 'Muzio fanatics' had booed the visiting diva. For the plaque's unveiling, the group arranged for the director's predecessor to deliver a lecture about Muzio and play some of her recordings so that they could 'hear her voice one more time at the Colón' (Benzecry, 2011, p. 119).

Over and above these ancillary episodes, Benzecry (2011, p. 126) argues that what draws fans to performances in the opera house is a 'quest for transcendence' that can be accomplished through several styles of engagement. The one labelled 'nostalgic' entails a past-centric orientation calibrated so that present opera experiences never measure up. What is striking about this category is that it is not generational; the nostalgic defends the belief in the superiority of the past not with personal memories but with 'technological evidence' (Benzecry, 2011, p. 136). In other words, recordings make it possible for operagoers under 30 to debate whether Maria Callas or Renata Tebaldi *is* (not *was*) the better soprano even though these fans are too young to have heard either singer perform when they were in their prime. In Benzecry's view, the nostalgic style of engagement contradicts Benjamin's (1969) expectation that the 'aura' of the work of art would wither in the age of mechanical reproduction; with opera, 'mechanical reproduction disenchants the present in such a way that the production of a unique and authentic experience (the meaning of aura) rests on the nostalgia for the live recordings of the past' (Benzecry, 2011, p. 138).

Taken together, the nostalgic orientation of opera fanatics and the commemorative rites they arrange for dead divas show that recordings can also function as relics by providing (as mentioned earlier) a 'kind of umbilical cord that connects the living and the celebrated dead' (Walsham, 2010, p. 13). According to Sterne (2003, p. 291), sound recording technology emerged as part of the nineteenth-century culture of preservation: 'recording was the product of a culture that had learned to can and embalm, to preserve the bodies of the dead so that they could continue to perform a social function after life'. In addition to preserving musical performances, recording technology also enables public and private acts of devotion by affording an 'acousmatic situation'

SOCIAL DEATH

wherein the departed musician's sound is heard but its cause remains unseen. This enables a different mode of listening in which 'sound is revealed in all its dimensions'; attention can be drawn 'to sound traits normally hidden from us by the simultaneous sight of the causes – hidden because this sight reinforces the perception of certain elements of the sound and obscures others' (Chion, 1994, p. 32).

Once it was possible for celebrated musicians to be heard in this way long after they died, performers were no longer spared from the 'anxiety of influence'. For example, once Ernest Lough's recording came to be seen as definitive, young singers shied away from Mendelssohn's 'Oh for the Wings of a Dove'; cellists adding the Elgar concerto to their repertoire do so under the shadow of Jacqueline Du Pré's recording with the famously exaggerated slide at the end of the opening phrase. Finalists in international music competitions are not only compared with the other competitors and the most esteemed concert artists of their time; jurors and audience members routinely compare them with their favourite recordings which can date as far back as the early twentieth century.

But eligibility for musical sainthood involves more than being remembered and admired after death; when it comes to the works required for this exalted status, composers have the advantage over performers. As Lang and Lang (1988) argue in their study of posthumous artistic reputation, survival in the collective memory depends on the availability of tangible objects, which is why artists who leave behind intact and durable original oeuvres are more likely to be remembered. Musicians who were mainly performers leave behind the instruments they have played (unless they are singers), and, if they lived in the right century, recordings, which document what they have *done* musically – the remarkable interpretations and technical mastery that garnered the praise of contemporaries. Musicians who were mainly composers leave behind scores, which may or may not have been lauded in their lifetime. What is more important is that these scores are thought to document their musical *intentions*, which performers feel morally obligated to honour.

The ambiguity of the score is commonly thought to weaken the composer's position because they must trust others to decipher their intentions and present their works in a compelling way. But this view is short-sighted. The necessarily cryptic nature of notation also allows for the composer's work to be made into an enigma, which is how the 'Beethoven effect' is initiated. It also grants composers a form of posthumous agency, in that their inscriptions spur subsequent generations on an endless search for what the composer 'really' wanted. While not all dead composers become saints, and the hierarchy of saints varies by region and over time, there is no question that composers serve as the central totemic figures in the elementary forms of musical life.

Acknowledgements

I am very grateful to Tony Walter, Jana Králová, Mary Hunter, Linda Gerstein, Dan Weiss and two anonymous reviewers for all of their insightful comments and suggestions.

Notes

1. Musicologists offer a more complex version of this narrative. See *Grove Music Online*, s.v., "Bach Revival" by Nicholas Temperley/Peter Wollny. http://www.oxfordmusiconline.com/subscriber/article/grove/music/01708 (Accessed 31 March 2015).
2. http://www.britten100.org/home (Accessed 31 March 2015).
3. *Grove Music Online*, s.v. "Schubert, Franz" by Robert Winter. http://www.oxfordmusiconline.com/subscriber/article/grove/music/25109. (Accessed 29 March 2015).
4. Wigler (1992). See also Kozinn (1992).
5. See also Ross (n.d.) and Ross (2014).
6. Unfortunately, the autopsy report has been lost, leaving the exact cause of death a mystery.

References

All-American Virtuoso. (1958, May 19). *Time*, p. 71.

Angenendt, A. (2010). Relics and their veneration. In M. Bagnoli, H. A. Klein, C. G. Mann, & J. Robinson (Eds.), *Treasures of heaven: Saints, relics, and devotion in medieval Europe* (pp. 19–28). Baltimore, MD: Walters Art Museum; Distributed by Yale University Press.

Ariès, P. (1981). *The hour of our death* (1st American ed.). New York, NY: Knopf.

B, J. (1892). Certain graves revisited. *The Musical Times and Singing Class Circular*, *33*(593), 393–394. doi:10.2307/3362781

Baird, J. W. (1990). *To die for Germany: Heroes in the Nazi pantheon*. Bloomington: Indiana University Press.

Beckerman, M. (2007). Introduction. In Michael Beckerman (Ed.), *Martinů mysterious accident: Essays in honor of Michael Henderson* (pp. 1–10). Hillsdale, NY: Pendragon Press.

Benjamin, W. (1969). *Illuminations* (pp. 217–251). New York, NY: Schocken Books.

Benzecry, C. E. (2011). *The opera fanatic: Ethnography of an obsession*. Chicago, IL: University of Chicago Press.

Boulez, P. (1986). Orchestras, concert hall, repertory, audiences. In J.-J. Nattiez (Ed.), *Orientations* (pp. 467–470). Cambridge, MA: Harvard University Press.

Bourdieu, P. (1984). *Distinction: A social critique of the judgement of taste* (R. Nice, Trans.). Cambridge, MA: Harvard University Press.

Bourdieu, P. ([1983] 1993). *The field of cultural production, or: The economic world reversed the field of cultural production: Essays on art and literature*. Cambridge, UK: Polity Press.

Burkholder, J. P. (1983). Museum pieces: The historicist mainstream in music of the last hundred years. *The Journal of Musicology*, *2*(2), 115–134. doi:10.2307/763802

Burnham, S. G. (1995). *Beethoven hero*. Princeton, NJ: Princeton University Press.

Chion, M. (1994). *Audio-vision: Sound on screen*. New York, NY: Columbia University Press.

DeNora, T. (2006). Music as agency in Beethoven's Vienna. In R. Eyerman & L. McCormick (Eds.), *Myth, meaning, and performance: Toward a new cultural sociology of the arts* (pp. 103–119). Boulder, CO: Paradigm.

Dimaggio, P. (1982). Cultural entrepreneurship in nineteenth-century Boston: The creation of an organizational base for high culture in America. *Media, Culture and Society*, *4*, 33–50.

Eisler, B. (2003). *Chopin's funeral*. New York, NY: Knopf.

Ekiert, J. (2010). *The endless search for Chopin: The history of the international Fryderyk Chopin piano competition in Warsaw* (A. Lloyd-Jones, Trans.). Warsaw: MUZA SA.

Figueroa, O. (1969). Argentina whistles for Sutherland. *Opera Magazine*, p. 57.

Fisk, J. (1994). The new simplicity: The music of Górecki, Tavener and Pärt. *The Hudson Review*, *47*(3), 394–412. doi:10.2307/3851788

Gal, S. (1991). Bartók's funeral: Representations of Europe in Hungarian political rhetoric. *American Ethnologist*, *18*(3), 440–458. doi:10.2307/645588

Gillingham, P. (2010). The strange business of memory: Relic forgery in Latin America. *Past & Present*, *206* (Suppl. 5), 199–226. doi:10.1093/pastj/gtq018

Halbwachs, M. (1980). The collective memory of musicians. (F. J. A. V. Y. D. Ditter, Trans.). *The collective memory* (1st ed., pp. 158–186). New York, NY: Harper & Row.

Harris, E. T. (1992). Handel's ghost: The composer's posthumous reputation in the eighteenth century. In J. Paynter, T. Howell, R. Orton, & P. Seymour (Eds.), *Companion to contemporary musical thought* (vol. 1, pp. 208–224). New York: Routledge.

Heinich, N. (1996). *The glory of Van Gogh: An anthropology of admiration*. Princeton, NJ: Princeton University Press.

Hunter, M. (2014). *Death, life and the performance of classical music*. Paper presented at the Performance Studies Network Third International Conference, Cambridge University, UK.

SOCIAL DEATH

Kanno, M. (2012). As if the composer is dead. *Mortality, 17*(2), 170–181. doi:10.1080/13576275.2012. 675197

Kozinn, A. (1992, June 25). Paderewski to go home, 51 years after his death. *The New York Times*, p. C16.

Kivy, P. (1993). Live performances and dead composers: On the ethics of musical interpretation. In *The fine art of repetition: Essays in the philosophy of music* (pp. 95–116). Cambridge: Cambridge University Press.

Lang, G. E., & Lang, K. (1988). Recognition and renown: The survival of artistic reputation. *American Journal of Sociology, 94*(1), 79–109. doi:10.2307/2781023

Laqueur, T. W. (2011). The deep time of the dead. *Social Research, 78*(3), 799–820.

Maier, H. (2006). Political religions and their images: Soviet communism, Italian fascism and German national socialism. *Totalitarian Movements and Political Religions, 7*(3), 267–281. doi:10.1080/14690760600819440

Margry, P. J. (2008). *Shrines and pilgrimage in the modern world: New itineraries into the sacred.* Amsterdam: Amsterdam University Press.

Musielak, H. (2003). La Mort de Frédéric Chopin. Le détournement de sa succession et ses conséquences. In I. Poniatowska (Ed.), *Chopin and his work in the context of culture* (pp. 77–95). Kraków: Polska Akademia Chopinowska.

Nettl, B. (1995). *Heartland excursions: Ethnomusicological reflections on schools of music.* Urbana: University of Illinois Press.

Petty, W. C. (1999). Chopin and the Ghost of Beethoven. *19th-Century Music, 22*(3), 281–299. doi:10.2307/746802

Pettyn, A. (2011). Chopin's Heart. In K. Sztarballo & M. Wardzynski (Eds.), *Heart of the city: Church of the holy cross in Warsaw* (pp. 147–151). Mazovia: Mazowiecka Jednostka Wdrazania Programow Unijnych.

Rosow, L. (1989). How eighteenth-century Parisians heard Lully's operas: The Case of *Armide*'s Fourth Act. In J. H. Heyer & J. R. Anthony (Eds.), *Jean-Baptiste Lully and the music of the French Baroque: Essays in honor of James R. Anthony* (pp. 213–237). Cambridge, NY: Cambridge University Press.

Ross, A. (2014, October 20). Deus Ex Musica. *The New Yorker, 90*, 44–49.

Ross, A. (n.d.). Chopin's Heart. *The New Yorker.* Retrieved December 10, 2014, from http://www.newyorker.com/culture/culture-desk/chopins-heart

Schiff, D. (2001). The man who mainstreamed Mahler. November 4.

Schütz, A. (1951). Making music together: A study in social relationship. *Social Research, xviii*(1), 76–97.

Service, T. (2015, January 12). This year's classical music anniversaries – and some less usual suspects. *The Guardian.* Retrieved from http://www.theguardian.com/music/tomserviceblog/2015/jan/12/classical-music-anniversaries-2015-nielsen-sibelius

Sherwood, S. (2006). Seeker of the sacred: A late Durkheimian theory of the artist. In R. Eyerman & L. McCormick (Eds.), *Myth, meaning, and performance: Toward a new cultural sociology of the arts* (pp. 81–101). Boulder, CO: Paradigm.

Sterne, J. (2003). *The audible past: Cultural origins of sound reproduction.* Durham: Duke University Press.

Straus, J. N. (1991). The 'Anxiety of Influence' in twentieth-century music. *The Journal of Musicology, 9*(4), 430–447. doi:10.2307/763870

Walsham, A. (2010). Introduction: Relics and remains. *Past & Present, 206*(Suppl. 5), 9–36. doi:10.1093/pastj/gtq026

Weber, W. (1984). The contemporaneity of eighteenth-century musical taste. *The Musical Quarterly, LXX*(2), 175–194. doi:10.2307/742209

Weber, W. (1989). The 1784 Handel commemoration as political ritual. *Journal of British Studies, 28*(1), 43–69. doi:10.2307/175417

Weber, W. (1994). Mass culture and the reshaping of European musical taste, 1770–1870. *International Review of the Aesthetics and Sociology of Music, 25*(1/2), 175–190. doi:10.2307/836942

Wigler, S. (1992, June 21). Pianist's body returns to Poland but heart stays behind. *The Atlanta Journal and Constitution*, p. B4.

Zerubavel, E. (2003). *Time maps: Collective memory and the social shape of the past.* Chicago, IL: University of Chicago Press.

Index

abandonment 17–18
abjection 30, 32, 34–5
absence–presence 55, 57, 59
admiration, anthropology of 92
advance care planning 41–3, 45–7
African-Americans, burial practices 7; *see also* slavery
afterlife beliefs 52, 55, 70–1, 95
agency: and the body 8–9; and communication 45; of the deceased 54, 95 (*see also* musicians, agency of dead); in dementia 33–4; in the face of care 32; in fourth age 28, 30, 34–5; and personhood 47; social withdrawal as 16–18, 23–4
agents: active 16, 23, 32, 41, 57–8; failed 34
AIDS *see* HIV/AIDS
alcohol 22–4, 57
alternative death entrepreneurs 76, 79, 84
ancestor veneration 52
anniversary programming xii, 7, 89–90, 93–5, 97
anxiety of influence 91, 99
art, sacralisation of 89, 91
artistic reputation, posthumous 99
authenticity 70, 90
autonomy 6–8, 29, 34, 52; patient 39, 42, 45
autopsy, sociological 18
awareness, open 44

Bach, J. S. 89, 93, 96
bad death 76
'bare life' 4
Barthes, Roland 62–3, 65–70, 72
Bartók, Béla 96
Beethoven, Ludwig van 91–2, 95–6
Beethoven effect 90–2, 98–9
being social 46
belief, experiential dimension of 71
Bernstein, Leonard 93
biological death *see* physical death
biomedical model of care 8, 30, 39, 46
birth control, enforced 11
body: disintegrating 1, 3, 8; foregrounding in social death 8, 46–7; powerful 8–9
Bourdieu, Pierre 89

Brana Plan 11
Britten, Benjamin 93
Buryat 52

candles, on graves 52, 66
care: dignified 45; moral imperative of 28, 31, 35; othering in 31; quality of 18, 38, 42–3; *see also* community care; EOLC (end-of-life care); palliative care; person-centred care
caregiving narratives 33–5
care homes 6, 32, 41, 43
carers: relationship with person cared for xi; and social existence of relatives 2, 7, 28; use of term 32
care services 25, 43
Castoriadis, Cornelius 29
charity 31
Chopin, Frederic 92–3, 97
citizenship 2–3, 34
classical music 7, 89–91, 95, 98
colonialism 31
coma 9
commemoration: of military deaths 80–1; of musicians xii, 7, 89–90, 93–4, 98; and suicide 77, 83–4
Communism 63–5, 95–7
community care 32
compassion 32, 34–5
composers: remains of 96–7; veneration of dead 7, 11, 89–91, 93–4, 96, 99
continuing bonds xii, 7–8, 50–9, 66, 68, 71
coroner records 18–20, 24–5
cross-generational links 2, 10
cultural assimilation 10
cultural capital 2–3, 5
cultural heritage 2, 7, 96
culture, falling from 8

Daniel, Roman Orthodox Patriarch 63–4
the dead: absence of 55–6; choosing relationships with 57; continuing bonds with *see* continuing bonds; and identity of the living 65–6; intimacy with 67, 72; phenomenological connection with 89; presence of 51–2; reconstructing biography of 56–7; special 96, 98; storytelling about 53

INDEX

death: different types of 1–2; marginalised causes of 78; professional taboos around 44; socially visible causes of 79–80; *see also* bad death; good death; lone death
death hierarchy 80, 84
death revival movement 78
death studies 2
dehumanisation 10
de los Ángeles, Victoria 98
dementia: and abjection 30; fear of 34; language describing 28, 32; perspective of person with 33–4; social death in xi, 2, 7–9, 16, 28–9, 32–3, 35
dignity 34, 38–40, 43, 78
disculturation 4
Disengagement Theory 5–6
divas, dead 7, 89–90, 98
dying: in care homes 43; changing nature of 41; communication about 44–5, 47; medicalised 45–6
dying alone *see* lone deaths
dying patients, medical attitudes towards 17, 42–7
dying trajectory 38

Easter, in Romania 64–5
emotions, in sociology 53
engagement, nostalgic style of 98
England: coroners in 19, 24; dealing with the dead in 52; EOLC in 38–41, 46
EOLC (end-of-life care): management of body in 46–7; origins of policy 40; patient involvement in 42, 44–5; and social death 8, 38–9, 41, 47; sub-groups lacking access to 43
euthanasia 38, 85.n1
'ex-human' 4–5

Facebook, deceased on 51
family-based social activists 78, 81, 84
forgiveness, institutionalising 71–2
fourth age xi, 28–31, 33–5
frailty: as 'black hole' 7; social construction of 30, 32, 34; and social death 33, 43
frame analysis 76, 78–9, 84

genealogical imaginary 54, 58
generations, succession of 68–9
genocide: as social death 2, 9–10; and well-being 11
good death: in EOLC policy 25, 38–40, 43; and lone death 17, 25
graves, mass 9, 96
gravestones xii, 7, 62–6, 68–9, 72
grief: disenfranchised 76–7; public 78; Western model of 51
grounded theory 79

Hancock, Sheila 35.n1
Handel, Georg 91, 93
healthcare culture 46
HIV/AIDS 5, 77–8

home, sense of 68–9
homo sacer 4–6
hospice movement 42
hospitalisation, long-term 4
Hurricane Katrina 11

iconography 70
identity: limitations on choice of 23–4; maintenance of 35; moral 29–32; use of term 4; *see also* social identity
identity support, reciprocal 68
illness experience 39; *see also* mental illness; terminal illness
inclusive exclusion 4
incontinence 30, 32
institutionalisation 4, 6
institutions: dying in 39; othering in 32; stigma of 4
intergenerational communication 58
intersubjectivity 11, 68, 94
interviews, accounts given in 53
isolation: and intergenerational communication 58; and social death 2, 41, 43, 51
Israel: military establishment in 80–1; and national death 84; suicide statistics in 81–3; suicide taboo in xi–xii, 5, 77–8, 80

Jackson, Adam xi–xii, 16, 20–5, 26.n1
Japan 51–2
Jews, in World War II 3–4
Judaism, suicide in xii, 76

Knesset 79, 82

Laslett, Peter 29
late-modern project 15, 23–4
legal protection, withdrawal of 2, 5
Lenin, Vladimir 9, 95
Lennon, John 97–8
liminality 2, 51, 55–7, 59
Liverpool Care Pathway 40, 43, 46
locked-in syndrome 7
lone deaths 15–20, 24–5

Mahler, Gustav 93
marginalisation 41, 78–9, 81–3, 85
marital bond, post-mortem persistence of 62–3, 69
Martinů, Bohuslav 96
mass imprisonment 11
material culture 7
memory: collective 10, 66, 68–9, 71, 94, 99; eschatology of 71; phenomenology of 68
Mendelssohn, Felix 93, 99
mental hospitals 4
mental illness 21, 92
meta-ethnography 3, 12
Mid-Staffordshire scandal 46
mind/body dualism 47
moral identity 29–32

INDEX

Morrison, Jim 98
Mozart, Wolfgang 91, 96–7
musicians, agency of dead xii, 90–1, 98–9; *see also* classical music; composers; divas
music-making, phenomenological analysis of 94
Muzio, Claudia 98

natal alienation 2
national death 84
National Socialism 95, 97
NHS (National Health Service) 40, 46
non-persons xi, 4–6, 50, 58
non-relationality 56, 59
notation, musical 94, 99
nursing homes *see* care homes

objects: in composer cult 90, 95 (*see also* relics); visual 70
old age: lone death in 18; social death in 17, 32–3; as social imaginary 30, 34; in the welfare state 31–2; *see also* fourth age; frailty
opera, death in 7, 90, 98
oppositional movement identities 82
Orthodox Church 64–5, 73, 95; *see also* ROC
ostracism 5–6, 76–7, 83
othering 30–4
Out of the Darkness Community Walks 77

Paderewski, Ignacy Jan 96–7
pairing 69
palliative care 38, 41, 43, 46
paranormal experiences 52
parenthood 6–7
Path to Life 76–84
patient choice 40, 42, 46
person-centred care 33–4, 39, 41–2, 46–7
personhood: elements of 42, 45–7; loss of 28–9, 33, 38–9, 45; maintaining 35
photographs: of the deceased 51, 66–7, 70–1; on gravestones xii, 62–3, 65–9, 71–2
physical death: due to social death 5–6; in EOLC 46; reframing 84; social connections after *see* continuing bonds; social existence, post-mortem; social death aggravating 10; social death before xi, 3, 5, 15–16, 23, 38, 41–2, 45
pity 31–2, 34–5
policy, as social agent 39
post-mortem *see* continuing bonds; social existence, post-mortem; social death, post-mortem
poverty 5, 11–12, 31
Presley, Elvis 98

Rachmaninov, Sergei 96
rape 4, 10–11
recordings, as relics 98–9
refugees 2–3, 9, 53
relatedness, everyday processes of 54

relational context 17
relationality: extraordinary 52; new 56, 59
relics, of dead musicians 7, 90, 95–6, 98
religiosity: fuzzy 63; modes of 70–2
remembrance 66, 95
rippling 55
rituals 52, 77
ROC (Romanian Orthodox Church) xii, 63–5, 70
Romania 7, 62–4, 72.n5; *see also* Vinerea

sainthood, musical 89–93, 96–7, 99
Schubert, Franz 96
scores, musical xii, 90, 99
self: loss of 33; mortification of 2; sameness of 35; transfer of sense of 69
self-harming 8
self-sacrifice 92
slavery 1–2, 4–5, 7, 50–1
snowballing sampling 53
social class 17
social connectedness, loss of 1, 3, 6, 12
social death: attempts to alter 79; conceptual framework of 3, 12; and death of spouse 67–71; demarcation lines of 9; for dying patients 45–6; extrusive and intrusive modes 2, 4–5; and imperative of care 32–3, 35; as miscommunication 44; other-perceived 2, 16–17; policy-makers' use of concept 39, 41–5; post-mortem 50–4, 56–9, 84–5 (*see also* suicide); self-imposed 15–18, 23, 25; self-perceived 2, 6; use of term 1–2, 16; and well-being 11–12
social degradation 62, 67, 69–71
social exclusion 2, 5, 76–7
social existence: as opposite of social death 2, 7, 10; post-mortem xii, 7–8, 15–16, 23–5, 54, 58, 83 (*see also* continuing bonds)
social identity: and the body 8; of the deceased 7, 24; loss of 1, 3–6, 12
social imaginary 28–31, 34–5
social life *see* social existence
social roles, loss of 4, 6–8
social vitality 9–11
social withdrawal, voluntary xi, 5–6, 15–16, 18, 23–5
'sociolization' 39
solitary confinement 6–7, 10–11, 51
Sontag, Susan 63, 66, 68, 70
spiritualism 51
Spivak, Gayatri 30–1
spouses, surviving 62, 65, 67–9, 71–2
stigma 4–5, 76–7, 82, 84, 92
storytelling xii, 53–4, 57–8
subalterns 31
Sudnow, David 1, 12, 41, 45–7
suicide: as agency 8; Durkheim on 5; ethnographic research on 18–19; in Israeli army 81; reframing 79–80; social death after 57, 76, 83–4; talking about 82–3; of Van Gogh 92

105

INDEX

suicide prevention 77–8, 80, 82
suicide survivors 76–80, 82–4
Sweden: as secularised country 51–2; storytelling about the dead in xii, 7, 52–3

taboo xii, 44, 76, 82, 84
Tchaikovsky, Piotr 96
terminal decline 29
terminal illness xi, 5, 18
threshold people 55
torture 8, 10
transcendence, quest for 98
Transylvania 7, 62, 64
tuning-in relationship 94

unemployment 6, 8
United States: AIDS activism in 77; suicide activism in 78; Vietnam memorials in 81

Van Gogh effect 92
Vincent, Joyce 26.n3
Vinerea 62, 64–5, 68, 71
Vita 5
vocalists, deceased *see* divas, dead
vulnerable persons 34

Wagner, Richard 90, 93
well-being 1, 3, 6, 9–12